HOPE AND SUFFERING

The Right Reverend
Desmond Mpilo Tutu

Hope and Suffering

SERMONS AND SPEECHES

*Compiled by Mothobi Mutloatse
and edited by John Webster*

*With a Foreword by
the Right Reverend Trevor Huddleston, CR*

WILLIAM B. EERDMANS
PUBLISHING COMPANY
GRAND RAPIDS   MICHIGAN

An edition of this book was first published by
Skotaville Publishers of Johannesburg in 1983
This edition first published in Great Britain
by Fount Paperbacks, London,
and in the United States of America
by William B. Eerdmans Publishing Company,
Grand Rapids, Michigan, in 1984

Reprinted, February 1985

Library of Congress Cataloging in Publication Data

Tutu, Desmond.
Hope and suffering.

1. Sermons, English.   2. Church of the Province of
South Africa — Sermons.   3. Anglican Communion — Sermons.
4. South Africa — Social conditions — Addresses, essays,
lectures.   5. South Africa — Politics and government —
1978-   — Addresses, essays, lectures.   I. Mutloatse,
Mothobi.   II. Webster, John.   III. Title.
BX5700.6.Z6T874   1984   252′.033   84-13686

ISBN 0-8028-1990-7 (pbk.)

This book is dedicated
to Nomalizo Leah Tutu

Contents

Foreword

The title chosen for this book of Bishop Desmond Tutu's sermons and speeches is singularly appropriate to the moment of its publication. "Hope and Suffering" is so clearly the expression of what he is preaching and speaking about when addressing the state of his own people in South Africa today. "Hope and Suffering" is so clearly, too, the expression of his own deepest Christian experience over the years and, more especially, the most recent years of his great ministry.

I have had the privilege of knowing Desmond Tutu for the best part of forty years. Our friendship began when he was a small boy and I was a young and inexperienced priest with responsibility for a vast African parish in Johannesburg. It grew and deepened when he had to spend long and weary months in hospital, and I would visit him and take him books to read, and always I would leave his bedside refreshed and cheered. The suffering was there all right because, with that exceptional intelligence and important exams awaiting him, he was frustrated and not a little lonely. But it was the *hope* that carried him so triumphantly through, and helped to carry me through with him. Those days and those visits are amongst my most precious memories of what was, for me, the golden age of my whole ministry.

But when you read the sermons, addresses and writings in this book you will certainly find hope and suffering intertwined in almost every paragraph. It is inevitable that this should be so for, as he looks out upon his country and speaks to its leaders, its people, its recurring crises and tragedies, Bishop Desmond looks out always in love and compassion. "When He beheld the city", we are told of Jesus looking out upon Jerusalem, "He wept over it" because of its refusal to know the things which belonged to its peace.

Here, in these pages, is the authentic voice of Christian prophecy in our day. Unafraid to proclaim with urgency the truth about "apartheid" as the evil and destructive force it is. Unafraid to challenge the Government and its representatives for their callous and sustained assault on human dignity and human rights. Unafraid to risk the consequences for himself in making such a proclamation. But *always* in hope: always in love: always in the certainty that God is present within the situation and that therefore His purposes must prevail. It is the delicious humour with which, even when speaking of the worst things, he conveys so unmistakably his own certainty about the future, that lifts the heart. There are too many instances of this to quote here, and in any case they should be read within the context of each address. But here is one example of what I mean (the occasion was the "celebration" of the twentieth anniversary of the proclamation of the Republic of South Africa in 1961): "What was there for them [the Africans] to celebrate? It was one of the most insensitive invitations of the many insensitive things to which Blacks have been subjected. They were being asked to celebrate their own oppression, their exploitation, etc. You might say 'But there are some good things that have happened', and we might concede that. The point though is that Blacks don't want crumbs of concessions from the master's table. They want to be there determining the menu together . . ."

For many months the South African Council of Churches, and Bishop Desmond as its General Secretary, have been subjected to fierce and determined scrutiny by a judicial inquiry known as the Eloff Commission. The purpose of this inquest was quite clearly to discredit and then to destroy the work of the Council, particularly its work in caring for the families of those victims of "apartheid": the detainees, the political prisoners, the people dispossessed by the population removals. During this time the pressures upon Bishop Desmond were tremendous, and included vicious personal attacks and the withholding of his passport. At the end of the day the Commission could find nothing which would justify any kind of censure for law-breaking. That in itself was a triumph in a country where legality and morality are so compromised by institutionalized racism.

Let me end this brief foreword by quoting from Desmond's submission to the Eloff Commission: "God's purposes are certain. They may remove a Tutu, they may remove the South African Council of Churches, but God's intention to establish His Kingdom of justice, of love, of compassion will not be thwarted. We are not scared, certainly not of the Government, or any other perpetrators of injustice and oppression, for victory is ours through Him who loved us!"

Thank God for this book and for each word in it! Now – READ IT!

Trevor Huddleston, CR

Bishop Tutu – A Biography

Bishop Desmond Mpilo Tutu was born on 7 October 1931 in Klerksdorp in the Western Transvaal, of a schoolteacher father and a relatively uneducated mother. He obtained his high school education at the famous Johannesburg Bantu High School (Madibane) in Western Native Township (1945–50). He followed in his "timer's" footsteps by obtaining a teacher's diploma at the Pretoria Bantu Normal College (1951–3), and in 1954 got his BA degree through the University of South Africa, teaching at his alma mater soon thereafter.

Between 1955 and 1958 he taught at the Munsieville High School in Krugersdorp, and during the years 1958–60 went for ordination training at St Peter's Theological College in Rosettenville, Johannesburg. He was ordained as deacon in December 1960, serving in Benoni Location the same year. By the following Christmas the man Tutu became Father Tutu. He had married Leah Nomalizo on 2 July 1955, and they celebrated their silver wedding anniversary in 1980.

Between 1962 and 1966 the Tutu family lived at Golders Green, in London, England, and he was a part-time curate at St Albans from 1962 to 1965, obtaining his BA honours in 1965, and his Master's in Theology, again in London, in 1966. Father Tutu then lived at Bletchingly in Surrey, where he was part-time curate at St Mary's, but at the end of that same year the Tutus *trekked* again, this time homebound, visiting the Holy Land along the way. He joined the teaching staff of the Federal Theological Seminary, Alice, in the Cape before it was expropriated by the Government. After that he lectured in theology for two years at the then University of Botswana, Lesotho and Swaziland, at Roma in Lesotho.

Then came another call from England . . . and so again the Tutus trekked. Father Tutu had been appointed Associate Director of the Theological Education Fund of the World Council of Churches based in Bromley, Kent where he was between 1972 and 1975. They lived in Grove Park, London where Father Tutu was the honorary curate of St Augustine's. Then came the break the dispossessed people of South Africa, especially Christians, had been waiting for . . . the historic appointment of the first Black Dean of the Anglican Church. The rest is history:

• Elected Fellow of King's College, London, in 1978

• Awarded an honorary Doctorate of Divinity from the General Theological Seminary, USA, in May 1978

• Another honorary Doctorate of Civil Law from the University of Kent at Canterbury, England

• Yet another honorary DCL from Harvard University, USA, in 1979

• Awarded the Prix d'Athene Prize by the Onassis Foundation in Greece, in 1980

• Awarded another honorary Doctorate of Divinity by Aberdeen University, Scotland, in July 1981

• Another honorary D.The. by Ruhr University, Bochum, West Germany, in 1981*

• Also the honorary Doctorate of Sacred Theology by Columbia University, USA

• Published a book of articles and reviews, *Crying in the Wilderness*, in the USA and Britain

---

* Not yet awarded personally as the Government has thrice refused the Bishop a passport.

- Bishop Tutu has twice been nominated for the Nobel Peace Prize (1981 and 1982)

11 May 1983   Mothobi Mutloatse
On the Way to Freedom,
Soweto

Desmond Tutu: Priest, Elder, and Prophet

Desmond Tutu is pɪ ncipally a pastor. His ministry stretches beyond St Augustine's church in Orlando West II (Mzimhlope), Soweto, where he is parish priest. It goes beyond the member churches of the South African Council of Churches, of which he is General Secretary, to embrace the whole of South Africa. Its impact reverberates around the world.

Desmond Tutu taught theology at the Federal Seminary at Alice (1967–9), and at the University of Botswana, Lesotho and Swaziland (1970–2), before becoming Associate Director of the Theological Education Fund in London (1972–5). He was appointed Dean of St Mary's Cathedral in Johannesburg from 1975 to 1976, and became the Bishop of Lesotho in 1976, only to return to Johannesburg in 1978 as the General Secretary of the South African Council of Churches (SACC).

There is something strikingly ordinary about this man, despite the purple he wears. When he appears in the 'township' gatherings, people strain their necks to have a look at him as if they had not seen him before. When he speaks they listen with eagerness as if they had not heard him before. He speaks with authority. And yet his speeches are interrupted by peals from the people whose faces lighten up momentarily at the expense of the White rulers, and he makes it clear that they are nothing but "dolled-up dwarfs".

This man possesses faith that dissipates fear, as he repeatedly encourages the Black people never to doubt that they will be free. For him, faith in God is an invisible pillar of strength. And so at every event where he participates, he acknowledges God's presence by saying a prayer, to the embarrassment of many a disillusioned Black who regards Christianity and its rituals as the handmaidens of the oppressive system.

There is no doubt that the credibility of Christianity among the politically radicalized Blacks owes a lot to his personal commitment. The Bishop sees the Gospel of Jesus Christ as "subversive of all injustice and evil" (*Divine Intention*, page 125). Prayer is therefore a dangerous exercise, for it reminds the oppressed of the Christ who identified with the rejected to the point of giving up His life for the liberation of mankind.

When he speaks, the hearts of the Black people burn with the desire to burst the chains of oppression. He courageously voices the groanings of the downtrodden whilst at the same time prophetically upholding the dream of the majority by calling for the "establishment of a non-racial but genuinely democratic society".

His enemies are longing for the day when news of his imprisonment will be announced. But then his international stature and the fear of an unprecedented upheaval at home restrains the Government from taking any drastic steps against him. Any such action could and would be interpreted not only as an act of persecution against the person of Tutu, but also against the Church of Christ where he has been consecrated as an elder and against the Black community whose dreams he embodies in his relentless fight against the apartheid system. The worst they could do to him is to kill him. But the Bikos and the Aggetts have gone that way. "Death", the Bishop maintains, "is not the worst thing that could happen to a Christian." He has, therefore, internalized the risks that accompany his discipleship.

The Bishop is deeply concerned about the broken

18

existence of the Black people. This is why he tirelessly calls for a common citizenship, the abolition of the Pass Laws and the forced removals of people, and a common educational system that will transform the quality of the entire South African society. He is, therefore, advocating a radical change in the laws, traditions and attitudes of the people of South Africa so as to build a common fatherland for all, irrespective of race.

In his pursuit for a common South African nationhood he is vehemently opposed to ethnic entities, be they Afrikaner or Zulu, that lay claim to an idea of nationhood that is little more than tribalism. It is this unwavering conviction that the foundations of the apartheid system must be dismantled that puts Bishop Tutu at the centre of a political storm. He openly acknowledges the authentic political leadership of those on Robben Island or in exile, and not the refurbished traditional leadership that owes allegiance not to the Black people, but to Pretoria. He defiantly champions the cause of the outlawed organizations which fight for a democratic, unitary state whilst disagreeing with their methods of achieving the goal of freedom. He has given his support to the "free Mandela" campaign, for Mandela, a legend in his lifetime, remains a living symbol of an alternative political order. He has called upon the world to exert economic pressure on South Africa, to the consternation of the White community and those Blacks who prefer to tolerate insults and enjoy the limited benefits of the system rather than suffer the pain of radical excision of the cancer of apartheid.

As an elder in that prophetic institution, the South African Council of Churches, over which the threatening sword of Damocles hangs, he, together with his co-workers, exercises a public pastoral ministry by supporting the families of the detainees, by giving spiritual solace to the families of the victims of the South African Defence Force (SADF) attacks, and by appealing for clemency on behalf of those who sought to gain freedom through violent means.

He has openly urged the churches to involve themselves unflinchingly in the struggle of the Black workers, as they collectively flex their muscles in demanding their right to bargain and uphold their dignity in a racist society, where Whites have grown fat on the sweat and blood of the Black working class. He has taken the side of the victims of the grand apartheid scheme as they are being uprooted from their ancestral homes to be dumped in areas where work is hard to come by, and where physical survival is well nigh impossible.

The Bishop has always considered this public pastoral ministry as being absolutely imperative in the Black community, where police harassment or victimization is the order of the day. This oppressive atmosphere has compelled people to sigh with grief within themselves, fearing to express their resentment or hate openly. In calling for and participating in commemorative services or personally attending funerals of the victims of apartheid, the Bishop has persistently sought to uphold the Black people's right to be heard. These public gatherings, always under close observation by the security police, are an expression of solidarity amongst the oppressed. It is in these gatherings that the charismatic Bishop evokes what J. B. Metz would call the "dangerous memory" of the evils perpetrated against the Black people. Tutu's public pastoral ministry simply poses itself as a bulwark of moral strength. From him the weak and the fearful draw strength as they are reminded of their collective responsibility to shrug off the chains of oppression. That is the only thing there is to lose. With the land expropriated, and the erstwhile inheritors of the land deprived of the very earth that guarantees them security, livelihood, a sense of independence and well-being – there is not much more to lose but to resist oppression with one's life if need be. This is the "subversive memory" evoked by the

Bishop. Not only does he remind the Black people of the irrevocable gift of freedom once possessed, of the fact that they were created in the image of God and therefore need not go through the Bureau of Standards or the Population Registration Office, manned by members of the oppressive White class; not only does he remind the Black people of the tradition of resistance that maimed and claimed the lives of many from the ranks of the downtrodden, but he also conjures a vision of certain victory over the forces of oppression, that these our oppressors will end up as the "flotsam and jetsam of history because the liberation God of the Exodus is always on the side of the underdog".

In the minds of the majority of the Black people Bishop Tutu stands in the grand tradition of the late chief Albert Luthuli, the late Mangaliso Robert Sobukwe, the imprisoned Nelson Mandela and others. These distinguished men symbolized and continue to symbolize the national aspirations of the Black people.

There is, therefore, a continuity between what the Bishop and the silenced Black leaders stand for. The goal is the same. But Tutu insists that he is not a political leader, although he is intensely involved in political issues. His involvement, however, does not recognize the "heretical dichotomy" between religion and politics. He is not a politician in the sense that his involvement is expected to lead to practical political reform only. His involvement aims at bringing about a changed moral order which transcends and yet upholds the anticipated radical political change. The apartheid system must be replaced, not just by a political order governed by a Black majority, but by a new order built on the foundations of justice. The means of bringing about this radical change must be "reasonably peaceful" (*Divine Intention*).

It is at this point that the Bishop emerges as a moral educator who differs radically from the political leadership

21

that either maintains the status quo through institutionalized violence or adopts violent means to overthrow the present unjust apartheid system. Tutu's stance is reminiscent of the position that was taken by Martin Luther King, Jnr, a position that cost him his life.

Many a radical Black person begrudges the Bishop for this disturbing moral stance. The deep scars caused by decades of exploitation and sheer terror have blunted the sharp edges of the Black community's moral sensitivity, hence the belief that violence is the only alternative means to achieve freedom. But this has not slowed down the Bishop in his advocacy of peaceful means. The temptation of compromising his discipleship is kept at bay. He is a firm believer that he is under divine compulsion to preach and actively promote the growth of justice in society.

> Speaking for myself, I want to say that there is nothing the Government can do to me that will stop me from being involved in what I believe is what God wants me to do. I do not do it because I like to do it. I do it because I am what I believe to be the influence of God's hand . . . I cannot help it when I see injustice. I cannot keep quiet . . .'

Therein lies the discontinuity between the moral leadership of Tutu and the political leadership of his fellow-travellers on the stoney road to freedom.

The Bishop's commitment to the value of justice has inspired him to call for the excommunication of the practitioners of apartheid (*Ecunews*, Vol. 8, 15 May 1981). Nobody has been courageous enough to put this into practice. But this has left members of the liberal White church with a feeling of discomfort.

Tutu believes in and promotes civil disobedience. Thus, in 1982, under his leadership, the SACC and other organizations gave financial assistance to help the 2000 Nyanga people defy their deportation order and return to the Eastern Cape. In 1981 he led a group of clergymen in a protest march against the detention of a fellow minister in defiance of the Riotous Assemblies Act. His repeated calls for economic pressure on South Africa have led the Government to deprive him of his right to travel outside South Africa, fearing that he will continue to embarrass the racist regime by exposing the evils of apartheid. This deprivation has not shaken his commitment to justice one iota. Not only has he kept in discomfort the White community that enjoys the benefits of apartheid, but he has also disturbed those Blacks who have been co-opted by the system to do its dirty work of promoting ethnic divisions, and has warned those Blacks who participate in the militarization of the land that they will be seen as traitors. Indeed, far from promoting the myth of unity within the Black community, he has laid bare the inconsistencies that plague them. If there is to be unity at all, it must be ultimately based on the value of justice.

Under such circumstances the question emerges as to whether the Bishop can be all things to all men. In a radically unjust society such a position is tilted towards neutrality. Thus he brings, not peace but a sword. The question of Black unity is just not on. Oppression alone cannot lay the true foundations of solidarity nor can its foster-sister Blackness. Dead wood cannot be "quickened" by being grafted on to a living branch. For those who have pledged their loyalty to the White dominant group in order to enhance their status and reap material benefits, the possibility of conversion, of turning around, borders on the miraculous. The march towards freedom cannot be delayed by attempts to persuade or even compel all Blacks to embrace a single ideological belief. A complexity of factors ranging from fear, the pain of sacrifice, the weight of "Kaffir mentality", to the luring material benefits etc., can dissuade people from opting for a "fundamental project" of total freedom.

Tutu's dilemma about unity does not stop on the threshold of the Black household. It extends to Whites as well. He heads the biggest ecumenical body in South Africa. His indefatigable pursuit of dialogue with members of the White ruling class bears abundant testimony to his commitment to unity. It is this commitment on the part of the Bishop that prompts the fervent adherents of Black consciousness to question the role of moderate leadership. Many a young Black is impatient with the likes of the Bishop, who pursues the question of unity to the point of risking his credibility. But Tutu, himself an exponent of Black consciousness, addresses the White community only to be a cause of dissension so that those within the White *laager* realize that a "man's enemies are those of his own household". Perchance this exercise in dialogue might strike home so that those who are brave enough to remove the veil of self-deception might be like a "briar" or a "hedge of thorn" within their own White community (Micah 7:6). The risks are high. But Tutu maintains that his mandate is biblical (*Divine Intention*). And so he even talks to the Pharaoh himself, relentlessly pursuing the model of Moses of the tribe of Levi. But surely the Bishop knows that the latter-day Pharaohs, like the Pharaoh of old, will not relent until they are overtaken by the merciless hand of violence.

From the above it is quite clear that for the Bishop, matters of faith cannot just be restricted to a "purely spiritual mission". Faith ought to have a bearing on the socio-political structures that maintain the Black people in a position of subjugation. Christian commitment therefore involves not only a critical reflection on the patterns of injustice in South Africa in the light of man's faith experience, but also commitment to realizing the dream of a just society. For him the Bible is the "most revolutionary" book. It is not a dead letter but alive. It exercises its power on those who believe by summoning them to remake history. Thus Tutu's theology is necessarily done within the horizon of faith. Without belief, theology becomes an irrational exercise devoid of an existential meaning.

He therefore becomes a theologican who points the way in a situation where injustice is rife, where the interpretation of scripture needs to be followed by programmes of action aimed at uprooting the apartheid system.

Tutu's critical reflection, courage and tireless efforts to realize a democratic and just society have been recognized by many Christian communities, individuals and organizations. He has been honoured with six doctorate degrees *honoris causa*, by six overseas universities.

Here in South Africa he has not yet been honoured. Perhaps the liberal White universities will honour him posthumously lest they be taken to task for recognizing a man who symbolizes and advocates a radically new political moral order. The Bishop cannot expect to be honoured by the Black universities that are either governed by Pretoria or that are loyal to the "homeland" leaders. He has been a consistent opponent of the fragmentation of the land on ethnic lines. Black universities fall under the enemies' sphere of influence. To recognize what Tutu stands for would be to contradict Pretoria. This the universities dare not do.

Thus the Bishop points towards the Church of the future, a Church freed from its dogmatic trappings and its denominational divisions, that are no less misleading than the ethnic divisions imposed by the apartheid system. He is the symbol of the Church that is concerned with justice and upliftment of the underdog. In order for the Church to inspire the building of authentic, caring human communities, it will have to disinvest from its numerous theological commissions and even abandon some of its traditional loyalties. The concerns of Bishop Tutu and many others mark a significant departure from the traditional pastoral ministry. Freedom must become a reality amongst the oppressed.

Father Buti Tlhagale

Father Buti Thlagale is a
Roman Catholic priest working in Soweto

CHAPTER 1

Introducing South Africa

1. **Open Letter to Mr John Vorster**
2. **Politics and Religion – The Seamless Garment**
3. **The Vineyard of Naboth and Duncan Village**
4. **Fortieth Anniversary of the Republic?**

Since Desmond Tutu arrived back in South Africa in 1975, to take up the post of Anglican Dean of Johannesburg, he has been preaching the Christian message of justice, equality and respect for people whatever the colour of their skin. The frank dialogue he has sought to promote (and a sober warning of the terrible nature of violence) is seen in his open letter to Mr John Vorster. His response to the allegations made in South Africa by supporters of apartheid – that he is "political" rather than Christian – follows. As a reminder of the every-day deprivation that apartheid creates in the lives of the Black majority "The Vineyard of Naboth and Duncan Village", a sermon preached in a township near East London, also shows how Bishop Tutu sees Old Testament history as relevant and hopeful in the South African context. Finally, in an analysis of the twentieth anniversary of the South African republic – really a celebration of twenty years of White minority rule – Bishop Tutu describes the continuing polarization of the Black and White communities, and sets out measures that could lead a future South Africa to show the world "what unity in diversity really is about". – Ed.

27

Open Letter
to Mr John Vorster

The Hon. Prime Minister Mr John Vorster   6 May 1976
House of Assembly
CAPE TOWN
8000

Dear Mr Prime Minister,
   This will be my second letter ever to you. In 1972 after I
had been refused a passport to take up a post as Associate
Director of the Theological Education Fund, I appealed to
you to intervene on my behalf with the appropriate
authorities. Your intervention was successful because, soon
thereafter, the then Minister of the Interior changed his
mind and granted me and my family our passports. I am
writing, therefore, optimistically in the hope that this letter
will have similar happy results for all of us.
   I am writing to you, Sir, in all deep humility and courtesy
in my capacity as Anglican Dean of Johannesburg and,
therefore, as leader of several thousand Christians of all races
in the Diocese of Johannesburg. I am writing to you as one
who has come to be accepted by some Blacks (i.e. Africans,
Indians and Coloureds) as one of their spokesmen
articulating their deepest aspirations, as one who shares them
with equal steadfastness. I am writing to you, Sir, because
I know you to be a loving and caring father and husband, a
doting grandfather who has experienced the joys and anguish
of family life, its laughter and gaiety, its sorrows

and pangs. I am writing to you, Sir, as one who is passionately devoted to a happy and stable family life as the indispensable foundation of a sound and healthy society. You have flung out your arms to embrace and hug your children and your grandchildren, to smother them with your kisses, you have loved, you have wept, you have watched by the bed of a sick one whom you loved, you have watched by the deathbed of a beloved relative, you have been a proud father at the wedding of your children, you have shed tears by the graveside of one for whom your heart has been broken. In short, I am writing to you as one human person to another human person, gloriously created in the image of the self-same God, redeemed by the self-same Son of God who for all our sakes died on the cross and rose triumphant from the dead, and reigns in glory now at the right hand of the Father; sanctified by the self-same Holy Spirit who works inwardly in all of us to change our hearts of stone into hearts of flesh. I am, therefore, writing to you, Sir, as one Christian to another, for through our common baptism we have been made members of and are united in the Body of our dear Lord and Saviour, Jesus Christ. This Jesus Christ, whatever we may have done, has broken down all that separates us irrelevantly – such as race, sex, culture, status, etc. In this Jesus Christ we are for ever bound together as one redeemed humanity, Black and White together.

I am writing to you, Sir, as one who is a member of a race that has known what it has meant in frustration and hurt, in agony and humiliation, to be a subject people. The history of your own race speaks eloquently of how utterly impossible it is, when once the desire for freedom and self-determination is awakened in a people, for it to be quenched or to be satisfied with anything less than freedom and that self-determination. Your people, against tremendous odds, braved the unknown and faced up to daunting challenges and countless dangers rather than be held down as a subjugated people. And in the end they emerged victorious. Your people more than any other section of the White community must surely know in the very core of their being, if they were unaware of the lessons of history both ancient and modern, that absolutely nothing will stop a people from attaining their freedom to be a people who can hold their heads high, whose dignity to be human persons is respected, who can assume the responsibilities and obligations that are the necessary concomitants of the freedom they yearn for with all their being. For most Blacks this can never be in the homelands because they believe they have contributed substantially to the prosperity of an undivided South Africa. Blacks find it hard to understand why the Whites are said to form one nation when they are made up of Greeks, Italians, Portuguese, Afrikaners, French, Germans, English, etc. etc.; and then by some *tour de force* Blacks are said to form several nations – Xhosas, Zulus, Tswanas, etc. The Xhosas and Zulus, for example, are much closer to one another ethnically than, say, the Italians and the Germans in the White community. We all, Black and White together, belong to South Africa against a visiting Argentinian side. The South African team won hands down, and perhaps for the first time in our sporting history South Africans of all races found themselves vociferously supporting the same side against a common adversary. The heavens did not fall. Is it fanciful to see this as a parable of what will happen when all South Africans together are given a stake in their country, so that they will be ready to defend it against a common foe and struggle for its prosperity vigorously and enthusiastically?

I write to you, Sir, because our Ambassador to the United Nations, Mr Botha, declared that South Africa was moving away from discrimination based on race. This declaration excited not only us but the world at large. I am afraid that very little of this movement has been in evidence so far. It is not to move substantially from discrimination when some

30

signs are removed from park benches. These are only superficial changes which do not fundamentally affect the lives of Blacks. Husbands and fathers are still separated from their loved ones as a result of the pernicious system of migratory labour which a Dutch Reformed Church Synod once castigated as a cancer in South African society, one which had deleterious consequences on Black family life, thus undermining the stability of society which I referred to earlier. We don't see this much longed-for movement when we look at the overcrowded schools in Black townships, at the inadequate housing and woefully inadequate system of transport, etc.

I write to you, Sir, to give you all the credit due to you for your efforts at promoting *détente* and dialogue. In these efforts many of us here wanted to support you eagerly, but we feel we cannot in honesty do this, when external *détente* is not paralleled by equally vigorous efforts at internal *détente*. Blacks are grateful for all that has been done for them, but now they claim *an inalienable right to do things for themselves,* in co-operation with their fellow South Africans of all races.

I write to you, Sir, because, like you, I am deeply committed to real reconciliation with justice for all, and to peaceful change to a more just and open South African society in which the wonderful riches and wealth of our country will be shared more equitably. I write to you, Sir, to say with all the eloquence I can command that the security of our country ultimately depends not on military strength and a Security Police being given more and more draconian power to do virtually as they please without being accountable to the courts of our land, courts which have a splendid reputation throughout the world for fairness and justice. That is why we have called, and continue to call, for the release of all detainees or that they be brought before the courts where they should be punished if they have been

31

found guilty of indictable offences. There is much disquiet in our land that people can be held for such long periods in detention and then often either released without being charged or, when charged, usually acquitted; but this does not free them from police harassment. Though declared innocent by the courts, they are often punished by being banned or placed under house arrest or immediately re-detained. How long can a people, do you think, bear such blatant injustice and suffering? Much of the White community by and large, with all its prosperity, its privilege, its beautiful homes, its servants, its leisure, is hagridden by fear and a sense of insecurity. And this will continue to be the case until South Africans of all races are free. Freedom, Sir, is indivisible. The Whites in this land will not be free until all sections of our community are genuinely free. Then we will have a security that does not require such astronomical sums to maintain it, huge funds which could have been used in far more creative and profitable ways for the good of our whole community, which would take its rightful place as a leader in Africa and elsewhere, demonstrating as it will that people of different races can live amicably together. We need one another, and Blacks have tried to assure Whites that they don't want to drive them into the sea. How long can they go on giving these assurances and have them thrown back in their faces with contempt?

I am writing to you, Sir, because I have a growing nightmarish fear that unless something drastic is done very soon then bloodshed and violence are going to happen in South Africa almost inevitably. A people can take only so much and no more. The history of your own people which I referred to earlier demonstrated this, Vietnam has shown this, the struggle against Portugal has shown this. I wish to God that I am wrong and that I have misread history and the situation in my beloved homeland, my mother country South Africa. A people made desperate by despair, injustice and oppression will use desperate means. I am frightened, dreadfully frightened, that we may soon reach a point of no return, when events will generate a momentum of their own, when nothing will stop their reaching a bloody dénouement which is "too ghastly to contemplate", to quote your words, Sir.

I am frightened because I have some experience of the awfulness of violence. My wife and I, with our two youngest children, stayed for two months in Jerusalem in 1966 and we saw the escalating violence and the mounting tensions between Jew and Arab which preceded the Six Day War. I was in Addis Ababa when there was rioting in the streets, a prelude to the overthrow of the dynasty of Haile Selassie. I was in Uganda just before the expulsion of the Asians from that country, and have returned there since and experienced the fear and the evil of things there. I have visited the Sudan, admittedly after the end of the seventeen years of civil strife, but I could see what this internecine war had done to people and their property. I have visited Nigeria and the former Biafra, and have seen there the awful ravages of that ghastly civil war on property and on the souls of the defeated Biafrans. Last year I was privileged to address the General Assembly of the Presbyterian Church in Ireland in Belfast – and what I saw shook me to the core of my being. We saw daily on television in Britain horrific pictures of the pillage and destruction being perpetrated in Vietnam: children screaming from the excruciating agony of burns caused by napalm bombing, a people rushing helter skelter, looking so forlorn and bewildered that one wanted to cry out "But is there no God who cares in heaven?" No, I know violence and bloodshed and I and many of our people don't want that at all.

But we Blacks are exceedingly patient and peace-loving. We are aware that politics is the art of the possible. We cannot expect you to move so far in advance of your voters that you alienate their support. We are ready to accept some meaningful signs which would demonstrate that you and your Government and all Whites really mean business when you say you want peaceful change. First, accept the urban Black as a permanent inhabitant of what is wrongly called White South Africa, with consequent freehold property rights. He will have a stake in the land and would not easily join those who wish to destroy his country. Indeed, he would be willing to die to defend his mother country and his birthright. Secondly, and also as a matter of urgency, repeal the pass laws which demonstrate to Blacks more clearly than anything else that they are third-rate citizens in their beloved country. Thirdly, it is imperative, Sir, that you call a National Convention made up of the genuine leaders (i.e. leaders recognized as such by their section of the community), to try to work out an orderly evolution of South Africa into a non-racial, open and just society. I believe firmly that your leadership is quite unassailable and that you have been given virtually a blank cheque by the White electorate and that you have little to fear from a so-called right-wing backlash. For if the things which I suggest are not done soon, and a rapidly deteriorating situation arrested, then there will be no right wing to fear – there will be nothing.

I am writing this letter to you, Sir, during a three-day clergy retreat in Johannesburg, when in the atmosphere of deep silence, worship and adoration and family services of the Lord's Supper we seek to draw closer to Our Lord and try to discover what is the will of God for us and what are the promptings and inspirations of God's Holy Spirit. It is during this time that God seemed to move me to write this letter.

I hope to hear from you, Sir, as soon as you can conveniently respond, because I want to make this correspondence available to the press, preferably with your concurrence, so that all our people, both Black and White, will know that from our side we have done all that it is humanly possible to do, to appeal, not only to the rank and file of Whites, but to the highest political figure in the land, and to have issued the grave warning contained in my letter. This flows from a deep love and anguish for my country. I shall soon become Bishop of Lesotho, when I must reside in my new diocese. But I am quite clear in my own mind, and my wife supports me in this resolve, that we should retain our South African citizenship no matter how long we have to remain in Lesotho.

Please may God inspire you to hear us before it is too late, and may He bless you and your Government now and always.

Should you think it might serve any useful purpose, I am more than willing to meet with you to discuss the issues I raise here.

Since coming to this Cathedral last year, we have had a regular service, praying for Justice and Reconciliation in this country, every Friday. And at all services in the Cathedral we pray:

> God bless Africa,
> Guard her children,
> Guide her rulers and
> Give her peace,
> For Jesus Christ's sake.

And:

O Lord, make us instruments of Thy peace: where there is hatred, let us sow love; where there is injury, pardon; where there is despair, hope; where there is darkness, light; where there is sadness, joy.

O divine Master, grant that we may not so much seek to be consoled as to console, to be understood as to understand, to be loved as to love: for it is in giving that we receive, it is in pardoning that we are pardoned, it is in dying that we are born to eternal life. Amen.

And we mean it.

Yours respectfully,
Desmond Tutu

Politics and Religion –
The Seamless Garment

A familiar remark which has become almost a parrot cry is "Don't mix religion with politics!" It is a remark which is made not because a politician in his election campaign introduces a moral or religious element. No, we almost always hear it when a particular political, social or economic fact of life is criticized as being inconsistent with the Gospel of Jesus Christ as most Christians understand it. Politicians and others will utter that cry if, for instance, someone were to say that it is unchristian to neglect the development of rural areas because the inhabitants of those rural areas will be unable to resist the temptation to emigrate to the urban areas, where they will invariably help to cause slums to emerge. They will often not be able to compete on equal terms for jobs with their city counterparts, and so they will swell the ranks of the unemployed. They won't be able to find cheap accommodation because there is no longer such a commodity in the city, and so they will be reduced to putting up some kind of shelter on any available space, and a slum will have begun. If the Church demonstrates a

36

concern for the victims of some such neglect or exploitation or denounces the widening gap in the country between the very few who are rich and the vast majority who are poor (a gap that seems almost always to widen rather than narrow), then the Church will be accused of meddling in affairs it knows very little about. This kind of criticism will reach crescendo proportions if the Church not merely provides an ameliorative ambulance service, but aims to expose the root causes; if it becomes radical (which refers to the roots of the matter) then it will arouse the wrath of those who benefit from the particular inequitable status quo. It could expose itself then to harassment and worse in its concern for justice, for an equitable distribution of wealth, in its call for the eradication of corruption, for an end to the abuse of power, the need to empower the powerless. And so when you work for a more just, participatory and sustainable society whose members share in crucial decision-making about the issues that are important for their lives, that is when you hear the cry, "Don't mix religion with politics!"

It is strange that this happens only when a particular socio-political and economic policy is denounced as being unchristian or unjust. If that same policy is described by religious leaders as being in accordance with Christianity, then there is no question in this instance of religious persons being accused of mixing religion with politics. The White Dutch Reformed Church (DRC) in South Africa for a long time sought to provide scriptural justification for the Nationalist Party policy of apartheid. Nowhere was the cry uttered that this was mixing politics with religion; whereas when other South African Christians declared apartheid to be abhorrent to the Christian conscience, then people were told that religion and politics belonged in separate categories and that it was wrong to mix them. We need to add in fairness to the DRC that one hears less and less today that apartheid

37

can be justified scripturally.

The same point about not mixing politics with religion or vice versa is made by those who think that religion does have a bearing on what happens in politics. These persons tend to have an attenuated doctrine of reconciliation and want to avoid confrontation at all costs – to speak about a neutral God in situations of conflict, of injustice and oppression. They say God does not take sides and so the Church should not take sides, but must be somewhere in the middle. In an attempt to exercise a ministry of reconciliation such people present reconciliation as an easy option for Christians, and they speak about the need to be forgiving, especially to the victims of injustice, without making a call for repentance by the perpetrators of the injustice and for a redress of the unjust system – they will do this to such an extent that profound Christian words such as "reconciliation and forgiveness" are rejected with contempt by the poor and exploited because they appear to want them to acquiesce in their condition of oppression and exploitation and powerlessness. It appears then as if Christianity is interpreted by those advocates as an anaemic reconciliation aimed at their domestication. It is forgotten that reconciliation is no easy option, nor does it rule out confrontation. After all, it did cost God the death of His Son to effect reconciliation; the cross of Jesus was to expose the sinfulness of sin when He took on the powers of evil and routed them comprehensively. No, just as there can be no cheap grace so there can be no cheap reconciliation, because we cannot cry, "peace, peace" where there is no peace.

We must, therefore, examine the biblical evidence to see what the scriptures say about liberation. Do they say God is concerned only about individual salvation and has no interest in the redemption of the socio-political and economic matrix in which individuals live? Does it say the world is religiously and ethically neutral and of no consequence to salvation and the final consummation of all things, that what happens in the market place, in the courtroom, or in Parliament is of no particular religious significance, and that all that matters to God is what is confined to the sacred sphere of the ecclesiastical? Does it say God is in fact not really interested too much in what happens from Monday to Friday but only in that which happens on Sunday, and that He does not much care about the plight of the hungry, the dispossessed, the voiceless, powerless ones – that He does not take sides? When two persons are engaged in a conflict and one of them is considerably stronger than the other, to be neutral is not just and fair and impartisan because to be neutral is in fact to side with the powerful.

Taped Message to the fourth Anniversary of the All Africa Church Conference in Nairobi, Kenya, which Bishop Tutu was unable to attend because the Government had withdrawn his passport after his earlier trip to Scandinavia.

The Vineyard of Naboth and Duncan Village

I want to tell a story from the Old Testament, a story that I am sure you have heard before. Once upon a time there was a king of Israel called Ahab. He had extensive royal lands. But next to his property lay the vineyard of a relatively unimportant man. His name was Naboth.

His vineyard was rather a nuisance because it split up the King's lands into at least two bits. The King was a reasonable man. He went to Naboth with a proposal: "Look here, Naboth, I want to consolidate my possessions and your vineyard is in the way of these plans. Look, I want to buy your vineyard. I will give you a good price for your vineyard, or I will exchange it for another of equal value elsewhere as long as I can get to put my land into one piece."

Naboth replied, "Haikona [oh no], sorry, Your Majesty. You see, this is my ancestral home. It is not just any old property. My family spirits are here. My ancestors have been buried here. I am part of this property and it is part of me; it is part of my children's life and they are part of it. I can't help you."

The King, being an Israelite himself, knew perfectly well what Naboth was saying and agreed in his heart with him. He knew that there was nothing he could do. Naboth had a right to the vineyard which nothing could take away, not even the king of the land.

Of course the King was disappointed by the answer he got from Naboth, so when he returned to the palace, he sulked and refused to eat. He first went to bed and turned to face the wall.

Then his queen, Jezebel, came along and asked, "What is the matter, King Ahab? Why are you sulking and refusing to eat the good food which I have placed before you?" Then the King told his Queen that Naboth had frustrated his plans to consolidate the royal lands. The Queen was quite flabbergasted: "What, you are sulking because one of your subjects, an unknown farmer, has spoiled your plans?" Now the Queen came from a different country where kings really were kings, that is, they did whatever they wanted to do. She thought that that was how her husband too should behave. So she told him, "Get up and eat. Don't worry, I will fix up everything so that you will get Naboth's vineyard. You are the king in this country and we won't stand for any nonsense from anybody."

Yes, she fixed up everything. She arranged a mockery of a trial where false witnesses declared that Naboth was a bad man. He had blasphemed against God and the King. For this crime there was only one punishment – death. So Naboth was stoned to death and the Queen told her husband the King, "Get up – go and annex Naboth's vineyard. He is dead and nobody will stop you doing what you wanted to do, and nobody will worry about what happened to Naboth, after all, he was just a nobody himself."

The King got up smiling and pleased that his wife, the queen Jezebel, had acted so energetically and effectively. He went to expropriate Naboth's vineyard – and then an extraordinary thing happened.

The prophet Elijah, God's messenger, met the King as he was going to Naboth's vineyard. God, said the prophet, had seen what Jezebel and Ahab had done to Naboth, and God was angry and would take the side of this unimportant man, Naboth, in this cruel act of injustice. God would punish Jezebel and Ahab and their children.

That is the story I wish to leave with you people of Duncan Village. In this country you are regarded as of no real importance. You are told by those who are powerful in the land that you must move from your property because they want it. It does not matter to them that you don't want to move. You, like Naboth, are saying that your homes and your sites are not just ordinary property. They are part and parcel of who you are. You have lived in uncertainty and anxiety. You were threatened with removal some time ago and so you were not sure that you could afford to improve or maintain your homes. This village is deteriorating. Your community is being destroyed. You are being asked to abandon your South African citizenship and take on that of Ciskei, another ghetto of poverty and a reservoir of cheap labour. And it is almost as if you are being stoned to death as a community, just like Naboth.

You are nobodies in this country, the land of your birth, and those with power think they can act against you with impunity and that nothing will happen to them.

Now I want to remind you, and them too, that God cares. God cares about injustice, about oppression, about exploitation. God cares and always takes the side of those who are trodden underfoot. God cares that they want to move you from pillar to post.

Injustice and evil and oppression will not last for ever. They have been overcome by God in the cross of Jesus Our Lord. As we protest the evil of your threatened removal we must do so knowing that victory is ours already. The authorities will ultimately fail because what they are doing is evil and against God's law. You must be strengthened to resist what is evil. I want to remind you of the dignity and peaceful resistance of the mothers and wives in Langa and Nyanga in the Cape, where this Christian Government and its officials are actually disobeying a direct and explicit law of God contained in the Bible: "Those whom God has joined together, let no man put asunder" – and yet the Government is contravening this clear biblical law by making married men into migrant labourers staying in hostels, and by refusing their wives the right to live with their husbands and the fathers of their children.

There is enough land for everybody in South Africa. It is just that some people are greedy and at the moment they are also powerful, and so they can satisfy their greed at the expense of others whom they think to be unimportant and without power. But these are they whom God supports. South Africa, please remember the story of Naboth's vineyard.

Duncan Village
East London
July 1981

Fortieth Anniversary of the Republic?

We have just had a celebration of the twentieth anniversary of the South African Republic that demonstrated more than anything else just how divided we are as a nation. Actually there is an axiom that has the validity of those of Euclid: on any major issue you can be sure that most Whites are to be found on one side and most Blacks on the opposite. When the Irish rugby players came to South Africa most Whites were in a seventh heaven of delight, but the Blacks by and large execrated the Irish. That position was true as well for the Springbok tour of New Zealand. Or if you like, when the South African Defence Force (SADF) attacked African National Congress (ANC) bases in Mozambique most Whites were cock-a-hoop and most Blacks were mourning. A last example: Whites will call the people on the other side terrorists, whilst Blacks regard them as freedom fighters in the liberation struggle. We could multiply examples. This should suffice to point up what is embarrassingly, indeed distressingly, obvious. We are rent asunder. How has this come about?

When the Whites came to South Africa they were welcomed by the indigenous inhabitants, who provided them with fresh fruit and vegetables and the land on which to grow them. At first they behaved like model guests, but with the passage of time they abused their hospitality. Now that is not how South African text books describe it. They will invariably tell you that Blacks stole the White man's cattle and the White colonists captured the Black man's booty. History, like beauty, depends largely on the beholder so when you read that, for example, David Livingstone discovered the Victoria Falls, you might be forgiven for thinking that there was nobody around the Falls until Livingstone arrived on the scene.

The upshot was that before you could say Andries Treurnicht, the Whites had grabbed a lot of the land. In short they were the masters and they intended keeping that position. Basically that has been the political history of South Africa: how Whites could maintain their position of privilege, based on the biological accident and irrelevancy of the colour of their skins. The corollary of White privilege was to keep the Black man in his place. Some White parties were subtle in this intention; others were not so subtle. The Nationalists came into power in 1948 by being blatantly racist, with their apartheid *Swart gevaar* tactics. They used the scare story of the picture, "Would you let your daughter marry this man?"

The Nationalists exposed the South African political game in its true colours. Blacks had no say whatsoever in the most important decisions affecting their lives. They had not been consulted when they were deprived of their franchise. Racism was entrenched and legalized in the Statute Book of our land. Blacks forming 80 per cent of the population were relegated to 13 per cent of the land. They enjoyed none of the rights that citizens take for granted in a democracy – they had to carry passes; they were subjected to influx control measures; they lived in segregated areas little better than ghettoes; they received a segregated education with glaring disparity in annual Government expenditure per capita between Black and White (at present it is in the order 1:10). Things were done for them because their omniscient masters knew what was good for them. What the Nationalists did in 1948 and subsequently was to make explicit and blatant what was implicit in the South African way of life. And in 1961 the Republic referendum was held. Again Blacks were conspicuous by their exclusion and treated as if they were nonentities.

What was there for them to celebrate? – It was one of the most insensitive invitations of the many insensitive things to which Blacks have been subjected. They were being asked to celebrate their own oppression, their exploitation, etc. You might say, "But there are some good things that have happened", and we might concede that. The point though is that Blacks don't want crumbs of concessions from the master's table. They want to be there determining the menu together.

I have wondered why we were made to celebrate a twentieth anniversary. Normally the milestones you tick off are twenty-five, etc. Is it because the powers that be realize there won't be a twenty-fifth (R25) let alone an R40?

I have predicted that we will have a Black Prime Minister within the next five to ten years. Now we could in fact have R25 and R40, but it won't be a republic rammed down the throat of an unwilling populace ruled by a White racist minority. Because my vision is of a South Africa that is totally non-racial. It will be a society that is more just. The Rule of Law – so shamefully abrogated in this republic hagridden by fear and anxiety – the Rule of Law will prevail again. There will be no arbitrary bannings and detentions without trial. There will be freedom for all (at present nobody is really free; nobody will be really free until Blacks are free. Freedom is indivisible. Whites can't enjoy their separate freedoms. They spend too much time and resources defending those freedoms instead of enjoying them). There will be a Bill of Rights guaranteeing individual liberty. There will be no enforced integration, which I abhor as much as I do enforced separation. I am an unabashed egalitarian and libertarian because God has created us freely for freedom. People in the new South Africa will matter and be seen to be of infinite value because they are human beings created in the image of God. There will be alternative forms of national service and conscientious objector status readily available. In fact we will not have conscription, because South Africa will not need to spend the astronomical sums on defence that it does now because we won't be the polecat of the world on account of the racist policies which the rest of the world finds so abhorrent.

We shall be free, about that there can be no doubt. The Black cause of liberation will triumph, must triumph because it is a just and righteous cause. God is on our side because He is always on the side of the oppressed. The only questions are *how* and *when* freedom will come. We want it now and we want it to come reasonably peacefully. Whites have to decide whether they want it all to happen by negotiation or through violence and bloodshed, giving us Mr Vorster's alternative too ghastly to contemplate.

As starters Mr P. W. Botha has to do only four things to defuse the situation, setting the stage for negotiation by the authentic leaders of all the sections of our population (for Blacks those on Robben Island and in exile):

- A commitment to a common citizenship for all South Africans in an undivided South Africa.
- Abolition of the Pass Laws – evenly phased to avoid chaos. They are the most hated part of a hateful system – and to lift all banning orders or charge those banned in open court and restore habeas corpus.
- To call a halt to all forced population removals.
- To establish a uniform education system.

These are moderate claims: South Africa is going to be a beautiful land with beautiful people. And we will show the world what unity in diversity really is about. We will have justice and peace and love and compassion and caring and reconciliation and sharing. Won't that be just lovely?

Roedean Symposium
Johannesburg
July 1981

CHAPTER 2

Liberation as a Biblical Theme

Chapter 2 focuses on the theology that underlies Bishop Tutu's public stance, showing how the book of Exodus – demonstrating the creativity and eventual salvation of the Israelites in exile – is relevant to the dispossessed Black majority, who have effectively been rendered exiles and outcasts in their own country. "Hope and Witness", an appraisal of modern biblical criticism, examines what this understanding means for the conduct of South African Christians today.

Bishop Tutu's "Address to Deacons" shows that the Christian path in South Africa today is by no means an easy option. Two events in South Africa in 1983 provide a backdrop to this passage: on 24 October clergymen and journalists at the scene of a forced eviction of squatters from shanty homes were "brutally assaulted" by South African officials,* and earlier in the year Father Timothy Stanton, CR received a six-month sentence in a maximum security prison for declining to reveal to a court details of a conversation with two young people held under the Internal Security Act. The

---

* *Church Times*, 28 October 1983.

chapter concludes with Bishop Tutu relating his theological understanding to the stance he believes the Church (including, and especially, the Dutch Reformed Church) should take in the face of apartheid. – Ed.

The Story of Exodus (1)

God spoke to Moses and said, "I am the Lord. I appeared to Abraham, Isaac, and Jacob as God Almighty. But I did not let myself be known to them by my name JEHOVAH. Moreover, I made a covenant with them to give them Canaan, the land where they settled for a time as foreigners. And now I have heard the groaning of the Israelites, enslaved by the Egyptians, and I have called my covenant to mind. Say therefore to the Israelites, 'I am the Lord. I will release you from your labours in Egypt. I will rescue you from slavery there. I will redeem you with arm oustretched and with mighty acts of judgement. I will adopt you as my people, and I will become your God. You shall know that I, the Lord, am your God, the God who releases you from your labours in Egypt. I will lead you to the land which I swore with uplifted hand to give to Abraham, to Isaac and to Jacob. I will give it you for your possession. I am the Lord.'" (Exodus 6:2–9)

In the book of Exodus we are told that a certain group of persons were slaves in Egypt, and that they suffered grievously as a result of their slavery. They were used as builders to build the cities of Egypt and perhaps those strange structures which are still to be found in Egypt today – the Pyramids. They engaged in all this hard labour for no pay at all, and, as you can expect, they used to lament and cry as a result of all this suffering.

Now the first and most important point is that God heard their cry and He saw their affliction. He revealed that He was a God who cares, even though He is in His heaven of heavens. He is very close to His people. Remember that, my dear friends – He hears, He sees.

They must have suffered for a number of years and it must have seemed as if He did not care, as if He did not exist even. But on that day He appeared to Moses and He showed that He heard, He saw and that He cared.

This passage tells us another thing – that He remembered. He was there from the beginning and He had had dealings with the ancestors of these slaves. He had promised their ancestors that He would give them their own land – but here were their children, exiles and slaves in a foreign land. What about the promises that this God had made? Were they just worthless? Had He forgotten? Was He faithless and not to be trusted? The passage answers emphatically, No! This God through centuries and centuries does not forget – He is to be trusted. His word has been tried in the furnace as silver is tested, and His word emerges as trustworthy. And so He told Moses that He remembered the agreement which He had made with Abraham and with Isaac and with Jacob, and that He would fulfil His promise to them. He would give them Canaan, the Promised Land, the land flowing with milk and honey. He would do that because He is a God who hears, who sees, who cares, who remembers. He is a God who can be trusted, He is a God who has been there from the beginning, who does not change – the same as yesterday, today and for ever.

But all of this was of no real importance for the slaves. When you are a slave what you want most of all is to be set

50

free, to be liberated. And so for the slaves, the most important word that Moses brought to them was, "I will rescue you and set you free from bondage." You and I know that God did do this wonderful work – He did set them free from bondage. He helped them to escape from their slavery in the mighty act of the Exodus. So we know another thing about God – this God – He is not just a talking God. He is not like Bishop Tutu who was warned by Mr le Grange, the Minister of Police, "Bishop Tutu talks too much and he must be careful." This God did not just talk – He acted. He showed Himself to be a doing God. Perhaps we might add another point about God – He takes sides. He is not a neutral God. He took the side of the slaves, the oppressed, the victims. He is still the same even today, He sides with the poor, the hungry, the oppressed, and the victims of injustice.

So let us remind ourselves again and again just what kind of God our God is. He is always there. He has always been there. He does not sleep or go on a holiday or take a day off. He is always there. So don't despair. No matter how long it may take or seem to be – He is there. He hears, He sees, He cares and He acts. He takes sides. We must not doubt that He cares and will act. We must not doubt that He will take our side and that He will rescue us and lead us out of our bondage, out of our slavery, out of our poverty, out of our suffering. He will make us His own people, to worship Him, and He is almighty. Nothing will eventually stop Him. Nothing can stop Him from doing what He will do because He is that kind of God. Remember that and spread this Good News about the God of the Bible, about our God.

But the passage has something else. It says the Israelites heard what Moses said about God, all the things that I told you just now. But they did not listen to him, they could not hear him because their spirit had been broken because of their cruel slavery. They could not hear. That is a terrible thing. Their slavery had dehumanized them. They had come to believe that they were not quite as human as the Egyptians. They believed that they were somehow inferior, second-class human beings. They had what we call a slave mentality. Now we know all about this, don't we?

We remember just how broken their spirit was because one day when Moses found two Israelites fighting and tried to intervene, they shouted back at him, "Who made you ruler over us? Do you want to kill us as you killed the Egyptian?" They were informers and you read that Moses ran away to the land of Midian as a result. We know just what this sense of inferiority can do to people. We develop a self-hatred and despise one another as a result. And we treat one another as scum. Have you seen how we drive in town and how we drive in Soweto? In Soweto we stop our cars anywhere because we despise one another and treat one another as of little worth. Nurses, teachers, ministers and their peers often treat fellow Blacks as if they did not count. Some of the songs that we sing say, "Come out and see the bride. She is White as a 'Coloured'." Or when a Black has done something to another Black, then as if to praise him he says, "You are my white master." We do not deserve to be liberated because we are so divided.

Liberation is costly. Even after the Lord had delivered the Israelites from Egypt, they had to travel through the desert. They had to bear the responsibilities and difficulties of freedom. There was starvation and thirst and they kept complaining. They complained that their diet was monotonous, and what is worse, many of them preferred the days of bondage and the fleshpots of Egypt. We must remember that liberation is costly. It needs unity. We must hold hands and refuse to be divided. The ruler always wants to divide and rule. We must know that before we reach our promised land there will be imprisonments, there will be bannings, there will be detentions without trial, there will be deaths in detention, there will be exile, there will be division and there will be treachery and disloyalty. We must be ready. Some of us will not see the day of our liberation physically. But those people will have contributed to the struggle. Let us be united, let us be filled with hope, let us be those who respect one another.

> With all this in mind, what are we to say? If God is on our side, who is against us? . . . Then what can separate us from the love of Christ? Can affliction or hardship? Can persecution, hunger, nakedness, peril, or the sword? "We are being done to death for Thy sake all day long," as Scripture says; "we have been treated like sheep for slaughter" – and yet, in spite of all, overwhelming victory is ours through Him who loved us. For I am convinced that there is nothing in death or life, in the realm of spirits or superhuman powers, in the world as it is or the world as it shall be, in the forces of the universe, in heights or depths – nothing in all creation that can separate us from the love of God in Christ Jesus Our Lord. (Romans 8: 31, 35–39)

The Story of Exodus (2)

Introduction: The Old Testament

You don't need to have an extensive knowledge of the Old Testament to realize that the most significant event or action was the Exodus. In this event a rabble of slaves were taught by those who had the ability to see below the surface meaning of events, those whom we describe as inspired. They were taught to see that God Himself had intervened on their behalf. This God had on His own initiative taken their side against Pharaoh and all his host and had routed their enemy as He led them out of their bondage, across the Red Sea and eventually to the Holy Mount of Sinai, where He had given them a law by which they had to order their lives in perpetual thanksgiving for that signal act of deliverance.

He led them out of slavery with an outstretched and mighty arm, through Moses, and was with them in the wilderness, feeding them miraculously for forty years with manna and quails, and giving them water to drink. He had freed them from slavery, from being a non-people, in order to make of them His own peculiar possession, His own people, His chosen ones, His royal priesthood. This gracious act of divine initiative and divine intervention was to be indelibly impressed on the corporate memory of Israel, so that from that time on they would see everything in their national history and that of the entire universe from the perspective of this signal event. It was for them the founding event of their existence as a people *par excellence*. It would be for them the paradigm for describing God's activity in human history. From the vantage point of the Exodus, the Jew would look backwards even to the creation of the universe – for God who had defeated the Egyptian Pharaoh so signally (the Egyptian gods, you will note, don't even merit a mention, such nonentities are they deemed to be) and had shown His supreme control of the powers of nature (He could turn the rivers of Egypt into blood, He could make the Egyptian day as dark as night; He could command lice and locusts to do His bidding whenever He so desired), such a God, their God, must surely be the Lord of nature as much as He had clearly demonstrated that He was indubitably the Lord of history. So the Exodus God must also be the creator God who brought everything into existence at the beginning out of nothing (*ex nihilo*) by the mere breath of His mouth, by His word – the transcendent God who merely needed to speak, "Let there be . . . and there was!" by His majestic *fiat*.

The Israelites experienced God first as the gracious God of the Exodus, who had chosen them to be His people long before they could have done anything to deserve being so chosen. From then on they extrapolated their experience backwards to embrace the beginning times of creation, and showed that their choice had been long planned for in the story of the patriarchs, especially in the call of Abraham (Genesis 12:1–3).

They understood the future also in terms of the Exodus. To be delivered out of the bondage of exile would be as a second but greater Exodus (Isaiah 52: 2–6).

The concreteness of the Exodus liberation
And the Exodus was not spiritualized or etherealized out of existence. For the Israelite it was a tangible action, datable, happening in human history, which could be vouched for by those who had witnessed and experienced it. It was a thoroughly political act by which God was first made known to the Israelites. Nothing could be more political than helping a group of slaves to escape from their bondage. For the Israelite, therefore, the liberation of the Exodus was not just a spiritual or mystical experience. It was highly materialistic and had to do with being protected from an enemy in pursuit, being fed when hungry, being provided with water to quench their thirst. But it also had to do with the religious and spiritual dimension of forging relationships with God. They owed their very being to Him and were bound in a covenant relationship with Him that excluded worship of other deities. They had precise obligations to meet in order to be His people – obeying His commands by showing a particular kind of behaviour in their community, summed up in the decalogue. They must be holy because their God was holy. They must be compassionate, especially to the stranger and the alien, because they had been strangers and aliens themselves in Egypt. The Exodus had to do with

their whole lives – political, social, economic, personal, corporate – they were liberated people whose entire lives must reveal this comprehensive liberation that they had experienced. And they had been liberated *from* bondage *for* the purpose of being God's people, His agent for the sake of the world. This liberation was total and would be shown in their material prosperity and well-being – described in the term *shalom*. It embraced both the spiritual and the material, both the secular and the sacred. The Israelites would not understand our obsession with dichotomies – for the writ of their God ran everywhere since He was Lord of the entire universe and Lord of all life.

So the Exodus loomed large in the consciousness of the Israelite. The Psalms constantly referred to it; when he read the Prophets he would find references to it; when he celebrated the Passover annually and renewed the covenant obligations he was reminded of what God had done for His people, and he celebrated his God as the great God of the Exodus, the liberator God.

The New Testament
It is not surprising to find the theme of liberation looming large as well in the New Testament. Jesus is but the Greek form for Joshua who led the Israelites across the Jordan into the Promised Land. The New Testament reader was expected to be steeped in the Old Testament and thus to recognize allusions and references even though these might be oblique or subtle.

What was not fully realized in the Old Testament would find complete fulfilment in the New. Matthew sees Jesus as a second but greater Moses who, as did the first Moses, gives a law from the mountain top, albeit a new law (Matthew 5–7). Luke, describing the transfiguration, tells us that the subject of the conversation between Jesus, Moses and Elijah had to do with the destiny He was about to accomplish in

Jerusalem. And Luke uses the Greek word *Exodos* to describe that event. It can't have been merely coincidental. The New Testament describes Jesus as entering the lists on our behalf against the Devil and his cohorts. The temptation story depicts Him as engaged in mortal combat with Satan, and the arena of their conflict is the world inhabited by God's children. This fight continued until Jesus triumphed so signally on the cross – "It is accomplished", a victory underscored by His resurrection and ascension. The Devil is the prince of this world who must be put to rout. Jesus can thus refer to Himself as the ransom (Mark 10:45) to describe graphically what He has come to do; the ransom is paid to release those who have been kidnapped.

It is the release and the cost of the release that this word ransom is meant to highlight. Captives have been set free, and those set free are the new Israel formed from the nucleus of twelve (recalling the twelve tribes of the old Israel) (cf. 1 Peter 2: 9–10). The Devil has overstepped the bounds of his authority by enslaving God's children; he is the strong man who can do this until the stronger man (Jesus) comes on the scene and deprives him of his ill-gotten spoils (Luke 11:21–22 and parallels). Those possessed by demons, those who are sick are the prisoners and slaves of the evil one until the Messiah (the Anointed One of God) comes. His salvation for them must mean their release from this kind of captivity, this enslavement. Thus in healing a woman on the Sabbath, Jesus justifies it by declaring that this daughter of Abraham had been in bondage for those several years and she must be set free (Luke 13:16). Jesus seems to sum up His ministry with the words from Isaiah 61 which He uses for His sermon in the synagogue at Nazareth (Luke 4:17–21). Again we see that this liberation is meant to be total and comprehensive. So the theme of liberation and deliverance is as characteristic of the New Testament as we have seen it to be of the Old.

It refers to the forgiveness of sins, to recovery of health,

to the feeding of the hungry. People are set free *from* bondage
to the world, the Devil and sin, in order to be free *for* God,
and to be fully human because Christ came that they might
have life in its abundant fullness. He has set us free from all
that has made us less than God intended us to be, so that we
could have a humanity measured by nothing less than the
humanity of Christ Himself – a compassionate, a caring
person, concerned more for others than for himself, ready to
demonstrate his love for his friends by laying down his life
for those friends as his Lord and Master did, willing to wash
the disciples' feet in an act of self-giving humility because he
has been bought with a price – not of gold or any perishable
thing but with the precious blood of the Son of God Himself.
The new law is the Law of Love and to serve this God is really
perfect freedom.

He has liberated us from the realm of darkness and
brought us into the kingdom of His dear Son in whom our
release is secured and our sins are forgiven (Colossians 1:13)
when He led captivity captive and, making an open show of
them like a conquering Roman general, ascended into
heaven, from where He has showered upon us all spiritual
blessings in the heavenlies (Ephesians 1:2–3) filling us with
His spirit, so that we are at peace with God because we have
obtained through Christ our acquittal, and there can no
longer be condemnation for us in Christ (Romans 8:1–2).

We now in the spirit enjoy the glorious liberty of the
children of God because we are accepted in the Beloved
(Ephesians 1:6); we are sons in the Son (Galatians 3:26), and
are no longer hagridden by anxiety for we know that the
Father knows our needs even before we express them and is
only too ready to supply them. If we ask He is ready to give;
for we are of more value than the sparrow, as the very hairs
of our heads are numbered (Luke 12:6–7, 22–31 and
parallels). We have received the spirit of sonship and have
ready access to the Father through the spirit in Christ

(Ephesians 2:18). The Spirit of Jesus is a new kind of spirit, not a spirit of bondage but one that enables us to address God as Father, Abba – Abba is the intimate form used by small children when speaking of their fathers (Galatians 4:6–7). We no longer obey the law of our lower nature but we are now moving in the realm of the spirit (where the Spirit of the Lord is there is freedom, 2 Corinthians 3:17), because to live at the lower level spells death (Romans 8:5–6, 14–17).

We have no anxieties any longer because we are as young children. We are accepted and affirmed by God and so do not need to prove ourselves to Him. We do not need to impress Him, for His love has taken the initiative – His Son died for us whilst we were yet sinners (Romans 5:6–11). We have full confidence in God, as children have full confidence in their parents. We have been set free and our liberation is total and comprehensive – it includes being set free from political, social and economic structures that are oppressive and unjust since these would enslave us, and make us less than God intends us to be. There is little about "pie in the sky when you die" in the Gospel of Jesus Christ, for, as Archbishop Temple said, "Christianity is the most materialistic of the major religions." You qualify yourself for heaven or hell according to whether you did or did not do certain thoroughly secular and "unreligious" (in the narrow sense) things such as feeding the hungry, clothing the naked, visiting the sick and the imprisoned because these are they whom Christ calls the least of His brethren (Matthew 25:31–46). There is nowhere that the writ of God does not run, for everything belongs to Him (Psalm 24:1). Caesar must be accorded what is appropriate for him, and God must have all – including Caesar's domain; otherwise there would be a part of the universe, of life, which did not fall under God's control.

Our task

In setting us free to be His children, God wants to enlist us in His service as co-workers with Himself in the business of the Kingdom (1 Corinthians 3:9); we are to labour with God to humanize the universe and to help His children become ever more fully human, which is a glorious destiny – you see, God created us in His image. It was not to animals or spirits that He gave this splendid privilege, and when He chose to intervene decisively in our affairs, He did not come as a magnificent and impressive or awe-inspiring beast or as a glorious spirit, but He became a human being (Hebrews 2:16). Thus our humanity is for ever united with divinity. We are temples of the Holy Spirit (1 Corinthians 6:19). We are God-carriers and ought to genuflect to one another as we do to the reserved sacrament in the tabernacle. Our destiny is just too wonderful for words – even angels wish to look into these mysteries of the divine love (1 Peter 1:9–12), this great love which has enabled us to be called the children of God (1 John 3:1–2). We are being changed from glory to glory (2 Corinthians 3:18) because we are transfigured into the likeness of Christ. It is not clear what we shall be, but when Christ is manifested then we shall appear as He is (1 John 3:2–3). This final glory will be such as to outweigh any present suffering and tribulation (2 Corinthians 4:16–18). Indeed our present suffering is a prelude to our sharing Christ's glory as we have shared His passion. Suffering can be transmuted and transfigured (Romans 8:18–23). Nothing can change the fact of our status as God's beloved (Romans 8:31–39).

Because of our security, we can follow in the footsteps of Our Lord and Master. We realize the truth that life comes only through death; true greatness lies in being willing to empty ourselves so that we can be exalted. Our standards become those of Christ and not those of the world. We are to be like the seed that must fall to the ground and die in order to bear fruit (John 12:23–26). It is by losing our lives for the sake of the Gospel, for the sake of others, that we shall gain eternal life (Mark 9: 32–33f; Matthew 10:37–39). We were created freely for freedom and when we are free we are able to set others free to be themselves, not letting them live up to our expectations of them, but remembering that God believes in them as He believes in us.

How wonderful it would be if we could relax in our acceptance by God, so that we could then be free to accept others, to affirm them, to exult in their goodness and beauty, in their gifts, without feeling threatened and jealous and inadequate, because we too have our gifts, our strengths, because we too are loved for ever by God. He created me because He loved me; He upholds me in being because He loves me and He will love me for ever and ever.

Anglican Students Federation Conference
Pietermaritzburg
July 1981

Hope and Witness

I Introduction

Genesis 1:1 – "In the beginning God . . ." These words come from the first creation narrative. You all know that there are two stories of creation, reflecting two ancient traditions. The older and sublimely unsophisticated one is the tradition which mentions Adam and Eve. Because this tradition uses the special name Jahweh for God, it is called the "J" or Yahwist narrative. We will have no more to do with it in this Bible study. Our concern is with the much later tradition. This tradition of biblical material shows a keen interest in matters concerning sacrifice and ritual, and because of this and other characteristics has come to be described as the Priestly tradition or "P".

Now just let us look at the "P" creation narrative, Genesis 1:1–2 and 4. You will have to take it from me that every scholar has declared that the Hebrew used in this account is of a most outstanding quality – indeed it is some of the best in the whole Hebrew Bible. That is the first thing we note. In contrast to the "J" account, where God is depicted as if He were like man, that is, anthropomorphically, e.g. creating man out of the dust of the earth as a potter moulding his vessel from clay, in the "P" account God's transcendence, His quite otherness, is emphasized. This God creates absolutely effortlessly, by His mere, or should we say, sheer *fiat*. He has only to speak and things happen: "Let there be light . . ." and there was light. He does not have to struggle; His majesty and power are unassailable. There is no being to compete with or rival Him.

And this God is there from the beginning. There is no speculation about His origin and even about the nature of divinity. No, there is no theogony. Quite staggeringly – in the beginning God . . .

And so we go from one day of creation to the next with the majestic movement of a great work of art, until we reach the climax when man is created. You can almost see God rubbing His hands in divine satisfaction – the proper joy and satisfaction of an artist when he puts down his brush or the composer his pen. "And God saw everything that He had made and behold it was very good" – the final divine imprimatur on this splendid work.

II Exile and creativity

Now the extraordinary thing about this outstanding piece of theological creativity, for such it is indeed, is that it was written during the Exile. Can you believe that? When we want to show off we speak about the context in which a biblical piece was written as its *Sitz im Leben*, i.e. its situation in life. Most of the Bible is contextual and occasional in the sense that it is written not in a vacuum but is addressed to a particular context and is *occasioned* by a particular set of circumstances. Now can you believe that the "P" account, with its sublime and transcendental theology, could have come out of the Exile? You know the Exile refers to the time when the Jews were most of them banished by the Babylonians to live in exile many thousands of miles from their beloved motherland. Some of us, like the Bishop of Bloemfontein and others, have visited Winnie Mandela in Brandfort, where she has been banished from her work and home in Johannesburg, in Brandfort being placed amongst people whose language she did not speak. We have been forced to give her Holy Communion in the street in this beautiful land of ours, this country which claims to be Christian. And others, like the Bishop of Pretoria and Father Leo Rakale, have visited Dr Mampela Rampela, banished from her medical work in King William's Town to somewhere near Messina. Others, like the Bishop of Kimberley and Kuruman, visited and cared for that saintly man Robert Sobukwe in Kimberley. And we know that exile is galling.

There are many exiles from our beloved country – the most recent being the school children from our Black townships and, oh yes, Brian Brown and his family who left last week on an exit permit.

Exile is galling. And it must have been more so for the Jews, for was Jerusalem not the Holy City with its Temple where God's presence was always assured? Was the Holy Land not their Promised Land? And now here they were, castaways from their beloved land.

They were surrounded on all sides by reminders of the Babylonians' victory over them. There were imposing statues of the Babylonian gods, and temples dedicated to them, and the Jews felt that they were very small beer indeed. Their God had let them down very badly, because in the theology of those days if a people were defeated it meant that their God too had been vanquished and made to bite the dust. The Jews must have felt so low they could have crawled under a snake.

And it is out of such a slough of despond that this marvellous theological tract arises and is addressed precisely to the Jews who were without hope. It is a tremendous credal statement, designed to keep the embers of hope in the breasts of the Jews from going out completely. And it is accomplished by a masterly piece of demythologizing because this account debunks and ridicules the Babylonian creation story called *Enuma Elish*. In the Babylonian story there are several gods and there is a whole business about their origin in all kinds of divine matrimonial transactions. But for the Hebrew there is and can be only one God and so – "In the beginning God . . ."

The Babylonian story described how creation results from a bloody contest between Marduk and Tiamat. The Hebrew says one God; well He does not have to struggle. He just speaks and things happen. (Let there be . . . and there is.)

The Babylonian story said man already had evil elements in his make-up from the beginning and was created to be the drudge of the gods. Not so in the Hebrew account – he is created very good like the rest of God's creation; he is created like his God and is created to be his God's viceroy on earth.

In Babylonia the stars and the moon and the sun were gods who controlled man's destiny and for that reason were feared. Well, in the Hebrew account they are hardly mentioned at all, and they are there to serve, not to control man.

This is a tremendous *tour de force*, to uphold the hope and faith of a people who felt quite down and out. The assertions of "P" seemed to be a complete nonsense – all this business about God's sovereignty and so on, when all the evidence pointed to the contrary. But in the end it was vindicated.

III Consequences for us

My friends, in our land today, hands and shoulders are drooping because we look around and we see no prospect of real change to a more just, a more open society with a more equitable distribution of the good things of our land. There is a gloom and despondency among Blacks and Whites who had hoped that things might be beginning to move in the right direction. Most Whites have decided to throw in their lot with the Nationalists and are really saying, "We are going to hold on to what we have and you will have to take it over our dead bodies." Blacks are growing more embittered, and the chances of reasonably peaceful and non-violent change are fast disappearing. Those of us who still speak of love and peace and justice and reconciliation are becoming discredited – and those who have worked for change and prayed for change are filled with despair and hopelessness.

And the Church of God must produce a relevant theology which speaks to this hopelessness and despondency. The Church of God must declare the Lordship of God and of His Christ – that God is the Lord of History and that this is His world despite all appearances to the contrary, that He is a God of justice and cares about oppression and exploitation, about deaths in detention, about front-enders, squatters' shacks, about unemployment and about power.

You know, there is another very interesting piece about the "P" story. You note that God finishes His work on the sixth day so that He can rest on the seventh – the Sabbath. Now you would have expected the Jews in this story to make out in a chauvinistic way that they were special to God from the beginning. I think one of the proofs that the Bible is inspired is such facts as "P" declaring that all the wonderful things He has said apply not only to the Jews but, wonderfully, to all men and women. So when we Christians speak prophetically, as we must, our truths must be spoken to all, Black and White, as is appropriate to each. There are many unpalatable truths that we must address to both groups if we are to speak for God.

IV *Witness, hope and suffering*
And if we do these things, uphold the faith and hope of God's people (who are all people on earth, not just Christians), then we must not be surprised that suffering will come our way. Let me not say this facilely; suffering has already come to many of our brothers and sisters. And it is almost the other side of the coin to witnessing. It is no accident that the Greek word for *witness* is the one we have taken over as *martyr*. To uphold faith and hope in these dark days of crisis is what it means to be the servants of God. Our servanthood and our witness are urgently necessary and must be translated into action hallowed by prayer, the sacraments, worship and meditation shot through and through with the Holy Spirit of God. I can't give you a catalogue of what witnessing spells out for you, but let me give you examples of things which if this country is to be converted and so survive we must begin to do urgently. I say urgently because I know you know that we have precious little time left. We are faced with a serious crisis.

We must have examples immediately that the alternative society which is the Church alive is possible and viable. It is important in a grasping, selfish society, for us to demonstrate in small or large church groups that it is possible for Black and White genuinely to share. We may have to run the risk of breaking the law – but I think they have told us that they would much rather obey God than man. And unfortunately too many have been brainwashed into thinking that legally right and morally right mean the same thing. It is illegal in this country for church groups to meet for more than a day without permission. It is eminently not immoral to do so. And this sharing of worship and insights and resources must not be only for special occasions. It must be our lifestyle.

We must counter half truths and untruths. It just won't do to be apathetic and allow others free rein. Freedom and liberty lose out by default because good people are not vigilant. We give up too soon and say the Government is too powerful. They are this because we have refused to stand up and be counted. We accept too easily Government propaganda about communism, etc. Have we thought for ourselves, "What is communism?" What has happened to dissent in this country? Why is it that Government officials can do things that in other countries would have led to their resignation, yet in this country they carry on regardless and with impunity? Are you satisfied that justice was done in the Joseph Mdluli case? In the Steve Biko case? Do you know that the man who was arrested with Steve Biko and who allegedly signed the confession which made Steve go berserk is now under Section 10 and will not be charged? Do you really care? Or it does not matter – it is Blacks. Or do you say that when the Government acts against someone there could be no smoke without fire? Beyers Naude is banned – do you really care, or do you say, "I always suspected that there was something fishy"? Do you care about the fate of all the banned, detained, political prisoners and their families? Do you know that the SACC, through its

67

Dependants' Conference (DC), spends 18,000 rand a month giving families of such persons (and there are over 600 families), at least 30 rand per month? Have you ever contributed to it or are you, like so many Whites, concerned not about the work of love and compassion carried out by Dependants' Conference but rather about the source of the funds, and really support those who burned the offices of the East Cape Council of Churches, and attempted to burn the flat of the young DC worker in Port Elizabeth? Why should Winnie or others be cared for by people coming from miles away – are there no local Christians who care? What have you done for, say, David Russell? Have you even sent him a telegram?

No, you don't want to be involved. Well, that is the crisis in this country and we must be compassionate and caring, and it will get us into trouble with the authorities because we are that kind of country already. But if we are the servants of the God and Father of Our Lord Jesus Christ then we can't be surprised that servanthood goes with suffering. Again out of the Exile someone wrote (thinking of Isaiah 61:1–3):

> We give thanks to God for the renewal that He is bringing to His Church through His Holy Spirit. But if we are filled with God's Holy Spirit, we cannot, in the view of the Bible, luxuriate in the experience of this Holy Spirit to enjoy it for ourselves. He does not permit this. It is He who was cast out into the wilderness to face the devil in mortal combat, and with words of a prophet of the period immediately after the Exile, this is what this spirit does when He possesses you . . .

Yes, there may be suffering, indeed there is already suffering, but if we are true to our calling then listen to what happens to the faithful suffering servant. (See Isaiah 53:10–12)

Dr Martin Luther King, Jnr said: "Together we must learn to live as brothers or together we will be forced to perish as fools."

I ask you, my friends, what do we want to do?

"In the beginning God . . . in the end God."

Hammanskraal
7 April 1978

Address to Deacons

My dear Brothers, you are being prepared for one of the most wonderful moments in your life – when you will be ordained priests. This means that you will have a special share in the one royal priesthood of Our Lord and Saviour Jesus Christ, the true High Priest of our faith who ever lives to make intercession for us, having entered the vale with the blood of His own all-sufficient sacrifice, which He made once and for all on the altar of the cross on Calvary. I want us to note a few characteristics which God, we pray, will help develop in your lives if you are to be effective priests.

Isaiah 42:3   Gentleness and humility
You know as well as I that the people of God will hold you in high esteem. They are wonderful, these congregations of God's flock, this precious possession of God which He bought with His own blood. The Ordinal will remind you constantly just how high your calling is, and just how valuable and important are the people you will be serving.

69

But they are always so keenly aware, too, of your importance and they will almost always treat you as if you were royalty. They will give you the best *rondavel* (hut) in the village, specially prepared for you. They will want to wait hand and foot on you because this is how they demonstrate their love to God for giving them a priest. They will cook you delicious meals provided from their valuable chickens and you must eat and eat, otherwise they will be hurt. But please remember that you are there to serve them. "A person is a person through other persons", we say, and, "A chief is a chief through his people." What is a priest without a congregation? He can't even celebrate Holy Communion without them. He is there because of them. Never forget that – you exist on their behalf to help them to love God better and so to serve Him by serving their fellow human beings. You are there to lead them and so you must love them. Our Lord loved His own, and having so loved them, loved them to the uttermost and so He took a towel and washed the feet of His disciples.

If you are full of yourself, then God can't fill you with Himself and with His gifts. My Brothers, pray that God will give you the grace to be humble – he who is exalted will be humbled and he who is humbled will be exalted. It will be difficult to be humble since the people in a real sense depend for so much in their faith on you. But you can grow in humility if you remember that you have nothing that you did not receive. All you have and all you are come from God. Don't be falsely modest. That is horrible. God has given you certain gifts. The people will recognize these gifts – intelligence, a beautiful voice, the gift of preaching, etc. Acknowledge your gifts and thank God for them. And yet remember always that they are gifts. "Why do you boast," asks Paul, "as if you have anything which you did not receive?" We all love a humble person and we detest a proud one, don't we? Attract others to God by your humility.

The message from Isaiah describes the qualities of the

servant of God, and the chief attribute here is gentleness. Let us watch our tongues. We can hurt, we can extinguish a weak flickering light by harsh words. Let us be always recollected and may God give us the grace to utter only those words of which we won't be ashamed afterwards, which we won't regret saying. It is easy to discourage, it is far too easy, all too easy to criticize, to complain, to rebuke. Let us try instead to be more quick to see even a small amount of good in a person and concentrate on that. Let us be more quick to praise than to find fault. Let us be more quick to thank others than to complain – "Thank you" and "Please" are small words, but they are oh, so powerful. My dear Brothers, please be gentle with God's people. It is so easy to put them off with harshness, and many could easily turn away from God because of a harsh or unkind word or attitude or deed. Be available for them. It is very taxing, it is very demanding – but that is part of the feet-washing, it is part of being the good shepherd who lays down his life for the sheep. If you are gentle and if you love them, the people will know it and they will accept your scolding because they will know it is all because you love them. And if you love them, they will do anything for you – I promise you. They are wonderfully appreciative and they don't forget. Care for them. I remember and will never forget how, when I was a server, our priest impressed me by always being concerned for us. At outstations he always saw to it that we were fed. That is something I will never forget. I try to do the same myself. So you see, you never know whom you may be influencing. You might get more vocations to the religious life and to the priesthood because somebody was impressed by the love and caringness of some priest. Enough about humility, gentleness, love and compassion.

Faithfulness and discipline

St Paul tells us that it is required in a steward that he be faithful. This is a wonderful relief to us. We are not expected to be successful. It would be intolerable if God demanded that we should be successful preachers, always able to fill our churches with our sermons, etc. I don't mean that we must have second-rate standards. No, we must give God only the best and, having done so, we must leave the results to Him. When we have done our best in our sermons, in our teaching, in whatever we do, then success or failure are for God to determine, and after all, God's ways are not our ways and it is always He who gives the increase. Success and failure are not as the world understands these things. But we must be faithful. This is where discipline comes in. We will largely be our own master even if we are under a rector. Only you can know whether you are keeping your rule of life concerning study, concerning prayer, and visiting and all the other things which we must do if we are to be faithful stewards and dispensers of the Word and Sacrament. You must have a timetable to which you try to stick for your study, otherwise you will find you will be caught up in so many other and very important activities that your study will go by the board and sooner or later your priesthood will suffer. Your sermons will become empty and hollow. This question of faithfulness is particularly important with regard to your prayer life. You are obliged to say the offices of morning and evening prayer, daily. Some priests have been known to be slack about this. You should be regular in your meditation, intercession and thanksgiving. It is crucially important, this. You are quite dead without prayer. The Son of God Himself was a man of prayer, as we note in the gospels. If it was necessary for the Son of God to be so prayerful, how much more must it be the case for us. God grant to you the grace to be faithful in prayer and study. I need not underline the importance of faithfulness in your pastoral work. You can sit all day in your house and not visit your people, not take communion to the sick, to the aged, and nobody will usually complain to you, but your church will grow emptier. You can't love people and not visit them. You can't love them unless you know them, and you can't know them unless you visit them regularly. And the good shepherd knows his sheep by name. All of us are hurt when people we have met before seem to have forgotten us. And we are thrilled and feel important if they remember our names. Yes, we are expected to be faithful and disciplined. And being disciplined means we will take holidays and breaks as well. Otherwise our bodies will go on strike.

Courtesy and long sufferingness
Humility and gentleness, which I spoke about earlier, go together with being courteous. Many of our people will be poor and uneducated but they are important to God. He died for them. He loves them. He knows their names. The very hairs of their heads are numbered. God did not say, "Be educated, be rich and be saved"; or, "Unless you are educated or rich you cannot enter the Kingdom of Heaven." No, He was quite clear in His own mind – "Blessed are the poor for they shall inherit the Kingdom of Heaven." It will be more easy for a camel to enter the eye of a needle than for a rich man to enter Heaven. So be warned. Respect them, because God does. Be courteous and don't bully them just because they will seldom answer back. God will answer back one day on their behalf.

When you are late for a service, it costs you nothing to say, "I am sorry I am late", and yet it will win you many friends. Jesus was very courteous to the sinners and the ones who were despised. Let us be so, too, with our people.

A last word. You will suffer as a priest. You will suffer when your people don't seem to want to co-operate and work with you. You will suffer when you see them suffering. You will suffer when you see their sinfulness. You will suffer with the burden of the churches. Yes, you may be called to suffer for them in prison and even by going to death. Greater love than this has no man, that he lay down his life for his friends. The Good Shepherd laid down His life for the sheep – but the way of suffering is the manner of saving the world. We each must share in Calvary and the cross, for only so can we share in the glorious victory of the resurrection. Only so can we participate in Easter. But first we must know Good Friday.

My Brothers, there is no more wonderful calling than the priesthood of the Church of God. May God bless you with His grace, that you may be gentle, humble, compassionate, faithful, disciplined, courteous and long suffering, to His praise, glory and honour.

Lesotho
December 1977

The Role of the Church in South Africa

Introduction – A Black Theology perspective
Before tackling the major subject, may I be permitted a few preliminary words on Black Theology which I wrote a few years ago.

"African and Black Theology are a sharp critique of how theology has tended to be done mostly in the North Atlantic world. Westerners usually call for an ecumenical, a universal theology, which they often identify with their brand of theologizing. Now this is thoroughly erroneous. Western theology is no more universal than another brand of theology can ever hope to be. For theology can never properly claim a universality which rightly belongs only to the eternal Gospel of Jesus Christ. Theology is a human activity possessing the limitations and the particularities of those who are theologizing. It can speak relevantly only when it speaks to a particular historically and spatio-temporally conditioned Christian community, and it must have the humility to accept the scandal of its particularity as well as its transience.

"Theology is not eternal nor can it ever hope to be perfect. There is no final theology. Of course, the true insights of each theology must have universal relevance, but theology gets distorted if it sets out from the very beginning to speak, or attempt to speak, universally. Christ is the universal man only because He is first and foremost a real and, therefore, a particular man. There must therefore of necessity be a diversity of theologies. And our unity arises because ultimately we all are reflecting on the one Divine activity which aims to set man free from all that enslaves him. There must be a plurality of theologies because we do not all apprehend the transcendent in exactly the same way, nor can we be expected to express our experience in the same way. On this point Maurice Wiles, Regius Professor of Divinity, University of Oxford, writes:

> Theology today is inductive and empirical in approach. It is the ever changing struggle to give expression to man's response to God. It is always inadequate and provisional. Variety is to be welcomed because no one approach can ever do justice to the transcendent reality of God. Our partial expressions need to be complemented by the different apprehensions of those whose traditions are other than our own. There are no fixed criteria for the

determination of theological truth and error. We ought therefore to be ready to tolerate a considerable measure even of what seems to us to be error, for we cannot be certain that it is we who are right. On this view a wide range of theological difference (even including what we regard as error) is not in itself a barrier to unity. ("Theology and Unity" in *Theology*, Vol. 77, No. 643, January 1974).

"Dr Ilogu can thus say there is 'a wrong premise that theology must remain an "unchanging doctrine"'. Vital theology, as the reflection upon the world, man and his activities through the Word of God, is at its best when it becomes living theology by becoming relevant to the age and time and the men living in them. Theology therefore must change from epoch to epoch and even from place and time to place and time. The fact of God's activities in creation and redemption through Christ, and in the sanctification of man through the Holy Spirit, do not change, but their interpretation and their application to man's situation do change (Ibid, p. 148).

"African and Black Theology must be concerned – and vitally concerned – with liberation because, as we have shown, liberation is a serious preoccupation at the present time and it is not seen as being an alternative to personal salvation in Jesus Christ. No, it is seen in Africa as the inescapable consequence of taking the Gospel of Jesus Christ seriously. Only a spiritually, politically, socially and economically free Africa, where Christianity today is expanding faster than anywhere else in the world, can make a distinctive contribution to the life of the body of Jesus Christ and to the world community as a whole. Of course, there are differences between these two kinds of theology and there must be differences because in a sense these two kinds of theology develop from different contexts. African theology on the whole can afford to be a little more leisurely though I am not convinced of this, because Africa by and large is politically independent but there is not the same kind of oppression which is the result of White racism in South Africa.

"Black Theology arises in a context of Black suffering at the hands of rampant White racism. And consequently Black Theology is much concerned to make sense theologically of the Black Experience whose main ingredient is Black suffering, in the light of God's revelation of Himself in the Man, Jesus Christ. It is concerned with the significance of Black Existence, with liberation, with the meaning of reconciliation, with humanization, with forgiveness. It is much more aggressive and abrasive in its assertions, because of a burning and evangelistic zeal, as it must convert the Black man out of the stupor of his subservience and obsequiousness, to the acceptance of the thrilling and demanding responsibility of full human personhood, to make him reach out to the glorious liberty of the sons of God. It burns to awaken the White man to the degradation into which he has fallen by dehumanizing the Black man, and so it is concerned with the liberation of the oppressor equally as with that of the oppressed. It is not so naïve as to think that only economic or political oppression are what matter. But liberation must thus be understood in a total sense as removal of all that which keeps us in bondage, all that which makes us less than what God intended us to be."

Nature gods and the God of nature and history
In ancient days, people were concerned about the fertility of their crops and herds. They wanted to be certain that the seasons would follow one another regularly, and that it would rain enough just when it should and that there would be sunshine when it was expected. Their gods therefore tended to be the forces of nature deified – the god of the rivers, the sun god, etc. – and basically they were nature gods whose

main function was to ensure that the steady round and rhythm of nature were uninterrupted. Spring, summer, autumn, winter, night and day, must happen in their proper sequence with no deviation. It is not surprising, therefore, that these gods were really gods of the status quo: this state of affairs is characterized accurately in Ecclesiastes 1:5–7, 9–10.

> The sun rises and the sun goes down; back it returns to its place and rises there again. The wind blows south, the wind blows north, round and round it goes and returns full circle. All streams run into the sea, yet the sea never overflows; back to the place from which streams ran they return to run again . . . What has happened will happen again, and what has been done will be done again, and there is nothing new under the sun . . .

Belief in these nature gods was a form of insurance for the prudent pragmatic man.

An utterly novel thing happened with the Israelite belief in Yahweh, a god who took human history seriously because it would be the arena of His self-revelation. "I will be who I will be" is a possible translation of the enigmatic name that He gives to Moses (Exodus 3:14–15; 6:2–3). The eye of faith of the one inspired by the Holy Spirit of Yahweh would discern the divine dimension in the ordinary events of human history and these events with a salvific significance would form salvation history – God acts in human history, often through human agents to save and rescue His people and through His covenant of mercy with them to bring them into His Kingdom of Shalom when all history would find its fulfilment, its dénouement in the *Eschaton* when God would be all in all, and the kingdoms of this world would be the kingdom of our God and of His Christ, and He shall reign for ever and ever (1 Corinthians 15:24–28; Revelation 1:1–15).

History, unlike the ancient Greek and Roman understanding, was not cyclic but moved towards an end, *Telos*, and so was linear, teleological and eschatological. It was open ended and not a deterministic or closed system, precisely because Yahweh was not a god of the status quo but a god who always took and takes the initiative to create new things, surprising things – that is His boast in Isaiah against the pagan no-gods, these empty vanities: "Let them come forward, these idols, let them foretell the future . . . let them predict things that are to be that we may know their outcome, declare what will happen hereafter; then we shall know you are gods" (Isaiah 41:22–23).

And of Himself He says: "Now I show you new things . . ." And in Revelation He declares, "Behold, I make all things new." He makes them so that history can achieve its consummation, which will be a paradise, as at the beginning when He created all things. Gunkel declared, "*Endzeit ist Urzeit*" (Isaiah 11:5–9; Revelation 21:1–4).

All this is set to happen because God, Yahweh, is a God of grace, of compassion and mercy. He is not a God far away or an impotent God. He is moved by the agony and suffering of His people and cannot be the Aristotelian unmoved mover dwelling in an unassailable Olympian height. No – listen, the Lord said, "I have indeed seen the misery of my people in Egypt. I have heard their outcry against their slave masters. I have taken heed of their suffering and have come down to rescue them from the power of Egypt and to bring them out of that country into a fine, broad land; it is a land flowing with milk and honey . . ." (Exodus 3:7–8). He did not just give sound advice, He came down and was involved in their misery and led them forth out of bondage into the freedom of the Promised Land so that they could be His people, His royal priesthood for the sake of the world (cf. Genesis 12:1–3).

This act of saving a rabble of slaves, this highly political act called the Exodus in the Bible, became a paradigmatic event, one which came to be seen as the founding event of the people of God, what constituted them His people, and other divine events were described in the light of this event, as the Christians later were to describe everything in their salvation history in the light of the death and resurrection event of Jesus Christ. God showed Himself there as a saving god, as a doing, an active kind of god, not one who was fond of delivering eloquent speeches, as a gracious god (they did not deserve to be saved, they could not merit being saved); and He showed Himself to be a god of liberation, the great Exodus god, who took the side of the oppressed, the exploited ones, the downtrodden, the marginalized ones. He was no fence-sitter. He took sides against the powerful on behalf of the widow, the orphan and the alien – classes of people who were often at the back of the queue, at the bottom of the pile. I could multiply biblical references to prove this point, e.g. . . . "He [God] is no respecter of persons and is not to be bribed. He secures justice for widows and orphans and loves the alien, giving him food and clothing. You too must love the alien for you once lived as aliens in Egypt" (Deuteronomy 10:18–20). The prophets waxed indignant at injustice and oppression in Israelite society because they were God's spokesmen, and such a god whom you could not really worship properly unless your socio-political conduct was consistent with your faith in Him:

> When you lift your hands outspread in prayer I will hide my eyes from you. Though you offer countless prayers, I will not listen. There is blood on your hands . . . cease to do evil, learn to do right, pursue justice and champion the oppressed, give the orphan his rights, plead the widow's cause. (Isaiah 1:15–17)

Or when God tells the Israelites He does not want their religious fasts:

> Is not this what I require of you as a fast: to loose the fetters of injustice, to untie the knots of the yoke, to snap every yoke and set free those who have been crushed? Is it not sharing your food with the hungry, taking the homeless poor into your house, clothing the naked when you meet them and never evading a duty to your kinsfolk?

This sounds almost like a version of Our Lord's parable of the last judgement in Matthew 25 – "Inasmuch as ye have done it to the least of these my brethren, ye have done it to me . . . Inasmuch as ye have not done it to the least of these my brethren, ye have not done it to me."

The God of Abraham, Isaac and Jacob, the God of our Fathers, the Father of Our Lord Jesus Christ was known then first as the God of the Exodus, the liberator God, and the theme of setting free, of rescuing captives or those who have been kidnapped, is one that runs through the Bible as a golden thread. It is an important part of the warp and woof of the biblical tradition. I have shown how central to the Old Testament tradition it is and will give a few examples in the New Testament.

Some New Testament evidence of the liberation Exodus motif
In the gospel according to Matthew we are constantly made aware of the Old Testament parallels in the New Testament. In fact this gospel is divided into five parts to reflect the five-fold law – the Pentateuch. Jesus is the Greek form of Joshua and he led the Israelites across the Jordan into the Promised Land. This second Joshua will lead God's people out of the bondage and wilderness of sin and alienation, we are being told in a stylized way, into the Promised Land of Shalom, of wholeness, that characterizes the Kingdom of Heaven.

Matthew makes Jesus out to be the second Moses who also goes up a mountain to deliver His law – the Torah of the Sermon on the Mount. It is quite inconceivable that Matthew, writing in a Jewish milieu, could have depicted Jesus as Moses the law-giver and separated this totally from Moses of the Exodus – because the law and the deliverance from bondage have an organic relationship in Jewish thinking. In Luke's gospel, we are told that the subject about which Jesus spoke with Elijah and Moses at the transfiguration was "His departure, the destiny He was to fulfil in Jerusalem" (Luke 9:31). The Greek word Luke uses for this departure is *Exodos*. Is this a mere coincidence, or does the word chosen have a theological significance meant to evoke the deliverance God wrought in Egypt, as giving meaning to that which Jesus would effect in Jerusalem?

The imagery of deliverance, of rescuing, of being set free – this imagery forms an important, indeed a crucial part of how the New Testament describes the saving and atoning work of Jesus. He Himself, revealing the terrible cost of redeeming us and effecting reconciliation between God and us and between ourselves, as well as with the rest of creation, speaks of Himself and His later work on the cross as a ransom for many (Mark 10:45;11). He inaugurates the Kingdom of God, His Father, by taking on the forces of the evil one. His mighty works of healing the sick, exorcizing the demon-possessed, opening the eyes of the blind and the ears of the deaf – these are signs to those who have eyes to see that the Kingdom of God has broken into human affairs. God has intervened decisively on the side of man. So Jesus is the strong man who comes to snatch back the ill-gotten booty of Beelzebub (Matthew 12:29–31). Being a sinner is like being a slave to sin, to death, to the Devil (Romans 6:5–13; John 8:30–35). And the truth and the Son will set us free, and we will be really free. Indeed the whole creation is travailing in bondage, longing for its release as it looks for the revelation of the glorious liberty of the children of God (Romans 8:18–22). Jesus is then depicted as He who is setting God's children free – so that it is imperative for Him to heal the woman crippled for eighteen years even if it must happen on the Sabbath, because this daughter of Abraham has been kept a prisoner by Satan in her infirmity (Luke 13:10–17). Ephesians and Colossians delight in describing Our Lord and Saviour as a conquering general who has routed the powers of evil and is now leading them in a public spectacle in His conquering hero's procession – He leads captivity itself captive and so can give gifts to us human beings (Ephesians 4:7; Colossians 2:15); we have been bought with a price (1 Peter 1:18; Acts 20:28) so that we are no longer our own; we have been made free to be a royal house, serving God as priests (Revelation 1:5).

The crown of all the New Testament evidence occurs in Christ's characterization of His ministry in the words of Isaiah:

The spirit of the Lord is upon me for he has anointed me. He has sent me to announce Good News to the poor, to proclaim release for prisoners and recovery of sight for the blind; to let the broken victims go free, to proclaim the acceptable Year of the Lord. (Isaiah 61:1–3)

And that acceptable year in the Old Testament was the Year of Jubilee, the year for setting slaves free (Leviticus 25).

In His ministry Jesus aroused the wrath of the religious establishment by hobnobbing with those who were called sinners, the prostitutes, the tax-collectors who collaborated with the hated Roman overlord and were despised for so doing (Mark 2:15–17). "He who has seen me has seen the Father" (John 14:7–10). He was revealing the self-same God who was biased in favour of the poor, the oppressed and the outcast, and Jesus ultimately died for being on that side.

83

I have demonstrated that the Exodus motif, the liberation motif, is deeply embedded in the biblical tradition. Then why are White Christians so flabbergasted when Black Christians invoke it?

Christian particularity

The reason in fact is quite simple. The Gospel of Jesus Christ is a many-splendoured thing, a jewel with several facets. In a situation such as in Ulster, the aspect of the Gospel that will be relevant there is the Gospel as reconciliation. If you are oppressed and the victim of exploitation then the Gospel for you will be liberation, and so on.

Black and White Christians look at Jesus Christ and they see a different reality. It is almost like beauty, which is said to be in the eye of the beholder. It depends on who and where you are, as to what is going to be pertinent for you. Then what is the role of the Church?

The role of the Church in South Africa

The Church exists primarily to worship and adore God. It must praise His most Holy Name. But it can never use this as a form of escapism. Precisely because it worships such a God it must take seriously the world He has created and which He loved so much that He gave His only begotten Son for it. Christians remember the strictures of the Old Testament prophets against an empty and formalistic worship. At the beginning of this paper we quoted examples of these prophetic denunciations. Jesus Himself reminded His followers that they could not offer an acceptable sacrifice on the altar if they had not been reconciled to their brother (Matthew 5:24), and the evangelist declares that anyone who claims to love God but hates his brother is a liar, because how can he love God whom he has not seen when he hates the brother whom he has? Our so-called vertical relationship with God is authenticated and expressed through our so-called horizontal relationship with our neighbour. Christianity knows nothing about pie in the sky when you die, or a concern for man's soul only. That would be a travesty of the religion of Jesus of Nazareth, who healed the sick, fed the hungry, etc. Christianity has been described as the most materialistic of the great religions. Jesus showed that for the spiritual God, His kingdom must have absolute centrality; but precisely because this was so, because He turned Godwards, He of necessity had to be turned manwards. He was the Man for others precisely because He was first and foremost the Man of God. If it must needs be so for the Son of God, it could not be otherwise for His Church.

The Church is constantly tempted to be conformed to the world, to want influence that comes from power, prestige and privilege, and it forgets all the while that its Lord and Master was born in a stable, that the message of the angels about His birth was announced first not to the high and mighty but to the simple rustic shepherds. The Church forgets that His solidarity was with the poor, the downtrodden, the sinners, the despised ones, the outcasts, the prostitutes, the very scum of society. These were His friends whom He said would go to heaven before the self-righteous ones, the Pharisees, the scribes, the religious leaders of His day. The Church thinks to its peril that it must sanctify any particular status quo, that it must identify with the powerful and uphold the system which will invariably be exploitative and oppressive to some extent. When it succumbs to the temptations of power and identifies with a powerful establishment, then woe betide that Church when that system is overthrown, when the powerless, the poor come into their own! It will go down with that system as happened especially to the Roman Catholics in Mozambique, and the Anglican Church in Zimbabwe and now the Roman Catholics in Zimbabwe.

85

The Church is always in the world but never of the world, and so must always maintain a critical distance from the political set-up so that it can exercise its prophetic ministry, "Thus saith the Lord", to denounce all that is contrary to the divine will whatever the cost. The Church has only one ultimate loyalty and that is to its Lord and Master Jesus Christ. The Church knows therefore that it will always have to say to worldly rulers whose laws are at variance with the laws of God that "We had much rather obey God than man" (Acts 4:19).

The Church must be ever ready to wash the disciples' feet, a serving Church, not a triumphalistic Church, biased in favour of the powerless to be their voice, to be in solidarity with the poor and oppressed, the marginalized ones – yes, preaching the Gospel of reconciliation but working for justice first, since there can never be real reconciliation without justice. It will demonstrate in its very life that Jesus has broken down the wall of partition, and so in its common life there will be no artificial barriers to any Christian being able to participate fully.

A Church that is in solidarity with the poor can never be a wealthy Church. It must sell all in a sense to follow its Master. It must sit loosely to the things of this world, using its wealth and resources for the sake of the least of Christ's brethren.

Such a Church will have to be a suffering Church, one which takes up its cross to follow Jesus. A Church that does not suffer is a contradiction in terms if it is not marked by the cross and inspired by the Holy Spirit. It must be ready to die, for only so can it share in Christ's passion so as to share His resurrection.

A grain of wheat remains a solitary grain unless it falls into the ground and dies; but if it dies, it bears a rich harvest. The man who loves himself is lost, but he who hates himself in this world will be kept safe for eternal life. If anyone serves me, he must follow me; where I am, my servant will be. Whoever serves me will be honoured by my Father. (John 12:24–26)

I pray that for the sake of our children, for the sake of our land and for God's sake, the Dutch Reformed Church will be converted to its true vocation as the Church of God, because if that were to happen, if it were to stop giving spurious biblical support to the most vicious system – apartheid – since Nazism, if it were to become truly prophetic, if it were to be identified with the poor, the disadvantaged, the oppressed, if it were to work for the liberation of all God's children in this land, then, why, we would have the most wonderful country in the world. If it does not do these things and do them soon, then when liberation comes it will be consigned to the outer darkness for having retarded the liberation struggle and for misleading the Afrikaner. That is my fervent prayer for my fellow Christians in the Dutch Reformed Church. Woe betide all of us if the grace of God fails to move this great Church, and all churches, to be agents of the great God of the Exodus, the liberator God.

Pretoria University
March 1981

CHAPTER 3

Current Concerns

1. **Population Removals**
2. **Black South African Perspectives and the Reagan Administration**
3. **The Role of White Opposition in South Africa**
4. **South Africa – Some Crystal-gazing**

South Africa's Black majority are barred from living in the affluent cities through a system of Pass Laws: they are forced into poverty in the "homelands", or into townships where they form the ill-paid labour force that services the White population. In his piece on population removals Bishop Tutu traces the progressive loss of the land rights of the Black population, through the establishment of apartheid by the Nationalist Party to the present day.

Bishop Tutu next describes how the advent of the Reagan administration in the USA firstly torpedoed the talks on the independence of Namibia, and secondly boosted the confidence of the practitioners of apartheid. The Reagan policy of "constructive engagement" has not, he argues, improved South Africa's appalling human rights record, nor has it led to any improvement in the lives of the Black community.

The dilemma of South Africa's White liberal opposition is discussed next. Should they participate in the South African parliamentary "charade", or should they walk out and take with them the only parliamentary opposition that there is? Finally Bishop Tutu assesses the possibility of reform in

South Africa, and renews his appeal to the international community to apply economic pressure on South Africa if they would like to see a peaceful resolution of the South African crisis. – Ed.

Population Removals

Historical preamble

Blacks have been pushed around really from the time Whites first set foot on South African soil. Those who came initially, to establish a halfway station to provide fresh supplies for the ships plying the lucrative Eastern trade, had among them those who wished to be more than just temporary sojourners. They decided to settle, build castles and take over large tracts of land with not so much as a by your leave. In addition they resented the indigenous people whom they had found in possession when they arrived and had now displaced. When these first settlers found British rule irksome, they ventured into the interior, capturing vast pieces of land through conquest because of their superior firing power. The constitutions of the Boer republics which they founded relegated the native peoples to a position of inferiority in State and Church.

This was hardly altered when Union came about in 1910, because what was previously done by means of the barrel of the gun now happened through the more sophisticated way of legislation passed through democratic processes. The effect was and has been the same – for the Blacks a progressive loss of land rights as the Whites amassed more for themselves, until we reached the position we find today entrenched in the 1913 and 1936 land laws, which decreed that nearly 80 per cent of the population would be confined to only 13 per cent of the land surface of the country of their birth.

1948 and after

When the Nationalists came to power in 1948 they resurrected their ideal of the Boer republics of the late nineteenth century and early twentieth century. They developed discriminatory legislation that was to hand, and initiated their own with amazing creativity – the Race Classification, the Job Reservation, Mixed Marriages, Immorality and other racist laws. But the apex of their achievement (or the nadir of Black deprivation) occurred with their Bantustan policy. Basically, the South African crisis is one that hinges on political power, for it is this, if you have it, which commands access to other kinds of power – economic well-being, social amenities and facilities. That is why it is such a charade to talk about improving the quality of life of Blacks in their own areas, in talking about the so-called changes which have been wrought in the matter of sport, the creation of international hotels and restaurants, in the removal of discriminatory signs. It is a charade because no matter how wonderful the improvements in the Black person's lot may be (and I don't doubt that there will be very significant improvements) these will always be mere concessions that are always at risk, and vulnerable because they depend on the whim of those who have political power. When they deem it convenient for themselves they will withhold these privileges and when they think otherwise they will dole them out lavishly, or not, from their bounty.

Basically it is a question of how you can maintain political power in the hands of a White oligarchy. Perhaps there is a preliminary stage – how do you, as a White minority outnumbered five to one, survive in a continent that has on the whole shown itself hostile to White presence? And the answer which the imperialistic Europeans decided upon with almost uncanny unanimity was to subjugate the native peoples and to retain most power in White hands. And so Africa in particular, but much of the so-called Third World in general, found itself ruled by these White foreigners. In time most of this colonial empire came to throw off the yoke of oppression. Southern Africa has been tardy in joining the liberation movement, but the waves of freedom have now washed away most White minority rule even in this sub-continent, the latest to fall being that in Zimbabwe, where we had famous last words from Mr Ian Smith, such as that it would not happen during his lifetime or only over his dead body and not in a thousand years.

During our period it has been quite clear that the Whites were determined to keep political power in their hands exclusively. It did not strike them as at all odd (at least, the majority of them) that the way they were going about things was totally at variance with the accepted meaning of that democracy whose virtues they extolled so much, as they vilified communism and Marxism.

On accession to power the Nationalist Party made no bones about their determination to maintain White domination with policies that were nakedly racist. They had stepped into the corridors of political power on the waves of White apprehension of the so-called Black peril, the *Swart Gevaar* ("Do you want your daughter to marry this man?"), and they did not conceal this from anybody. They used blatantly and deliberately discourteous terms when referring to Blacks, to the extent of saying they would not call us Mr, etc. And no "Dear Sirs" but greetings – Koelies, Hotnots and Kaffirs, were very much the order of the day. Even our English newspapers became part of this denignatory process. For instance, they would describe an accident in these

words: "Three persons and a Native were injured." We read
these things and they are etched in our memories. This was
just a part of the South African way of life – you knew that
to walk on the pavements of our cities meant you were sure
to be elbowed out of the way by your White masters. It was
part of this whole system of keeping the native in his place.

Dr Verwoerd at least had the virtue of honesty. When he
introduced Bantu Education he did not try to sell us all this
highfalutin stuff that we are getting from the apologists for
the system. He was clear in his own mind that Blacks should
not be educated above certain levels which would enable
them to be good servants of the Whites. And they should not
be misled into thinking that the green pastures on the White
side would ever be accessible to them.

They enforced the 1913 and 1936 land allocation
provisions vigorously. Blacks had never had any illusions
about their position and status in South Africa. They were
third-class inhabitants, not citizens in the land of their
forefathers. The laws at every turn proved this. But before
1948 Blacks had been lulled into a false expectancy. You see,
our fathers and brothers had died in the 1914–18 war to end
all wars; they had died in the 1939–45 war against Nazism
and fascism, and they believed that a new era of justice,
righteousness and peace was about to dawn for them and
their children too. Black Africans had lost their franchise in
the Cape and could no longer be directly represented in
Parliament. But they noted that so-called Coloureds were
still on the Common Voters Roll, and perhaps this right-
privilege would be extended to other Blacks in time. And to
demonstrate their law-abiding nature and their desire to
participate in the decision-making processes of their land,
they were willing to serve on dummy bodies such as the
location Advisory Boards, the Natives' Representative
Council, etc. They protested peacefully, they drew up
petitions, they went on delegations, they boycotted, they

engaged in passive resistance campaigns – all to no avail.

The Nationalists, in the first flush of electoral success, did not mince their words, nor were they gentle in their actions. They moved the people of Sophiatown and raped them of their freehold title rights. They killed a lively community. I know, for I lived in Sophiatown, in Meyer Street where the Community of the Resurrection had their house, headed by Bishop Trevor Huddleston. I remember that on the eve of my ordination to the priesthood, the then Bishop of Johannesburg, Leslie Stradling, took some of us to a confirmation service in the old Christ The King Church, which stood like a sentinel on a knoll towering over all of Sophiatown. But it was not the Sophiatown I had known. This was now a devastated area, with many houses razed to the ground and weeds growing rampant all over. It was so like a bombed-out area. That had been done to maintain White supremacy.

In those early days of unadulterated apartheid Dr Verwoerd found that the Minister of Education had introduced school feeding into Black schools. I recall as a small boy in the Afrikaner *dorpie* of Ventersdorp seeing White children throw into dustbins what they were given for school feeding – perfectly good sandwiches and fruit. They preferred the lunches their mothers had prepared for them. And I remember also another sight – that of Black children from the location (as they were called in those days) scavenging in the White school dustbins. I used to wonder how it was that children from the relatively well-off sector should be the ones who were fed, while those whose parents could least afford it financially and the children who could least afford it physically, were not fed. (I know some would say their parents paid taxes. I thought that our parents paid too but from a lower level of income, and in any case it wasn't their fault that they were paid low wages and so could not afford to pay high taxes.)

Well, when Dr Verwoerd found there was school feeding for most Black school children, he decided to put an end to it all. They have done some quite breathtaking things in their time, these Nationalists, but I think Dr Verwoerd's reason for stopping school feeding in Black schools still takes the cake. He said that since we could feed only some and not all, we must not feed even those we could. The cynicism of this statement is quite horrendous. Because you can't cure all TB patients don't cure those you can – would that be acceptable?

I quote all of this only to point out that the Nationalists at one time were not concerned to hide the fact that they were looking after the interests of only one group in this country – and that group wasn't the Blacks. And they did not hide this behind highfalutin convoluted statements or arguments. The White man was the top dog, and the Black was the underdog and they were going to see that it stayed that way.

They could not, however, pretend that they did not belong to a wider, a world community. Mr Eric Louw tended to find his sorties to the United Nations somewhat uncomfortable, and the criticism from the world was strident. The Nationalists decided that they would have to make their obviously racist and immoral policies appear less so, to make them more acceptable, in order also to help salve the consciences of those countries overseas which were investing in South Africa and profiting from cheap Black labour, from migratory labour, and benefiting so openly from Black misery. And that is the rationale for the new thrust in the developing of the Bantustans and in trying to encourage the use of separate development to describe their policy, rather than apartheid which had entered the world's vocabulary as something no decent person wanted to be seen dead with.

They really believed, and still believe, what they say. The Blacks (who were not consulted at all in any meaningful way about a policy that was shoved down our throats) would be able to exercise their political and other rights and freedoms in their own areas, arbitrarily carved up for them by the all mighty White Government who always, of course, had the interests of Blacks at heart. The Bantu (Plurals, Co-operatives, Blacks) did not form one single community. They were a conglomerate of several "nations" – Zulu, Xhosa, Tswana, etc., who would each be given their own Bantustan homeland, and the intention was that they would ultimately all "end up as autonomous sovereign nations". Never mind that the Xhosas presented us with the extraordinary phenomenon of being split into two groups or "nations" – the Transkeians and the Ciskeians. Never mind that nobody had explained, or has yet explained, by what *tour de force* the White community, with such diverse elements in it (Greeks, Swedes, English, Afrikaners), coalesced to form one nation. Never mind that apart from the Transkei none of these creations had territorial integrity or any hope of economic viability.

That was not the point – the point was how you could give a semblance of morality to something that had been condemned as evil. And that is the solution White South Africa has decided on for the vexed question of political power and co-existence in this part of the sub-continent. They have decided that it will happen only with power firmly in their grasp, and it will be co-existence only on the terms dictated by them. This means that there is to be a White South Africa, about whose precise delimitation the Whites alone will decide; and only Whites will be citizens of this part of South Africa, which could well be the most prosperous and most developed parts of our common fatherland. That might just be coincidental, but most of the cities, the mines and the ports will be part of this affluent section. Coloureds and Indians will almost certainly be co-opted to swell the numbers against the Black hordes.

And the Total Strategy is a developing one. Some very specially blessed Blacks (urban Blacks) will also be part of this "gravy train". Their quality of life will be significantly enhanced, their children are likely to go to good White schools, they will get very good salaries, etc. etc., and they will be co-opted into the system as a Black middle class to be a buffer between the *have*-Whites and the *have-not*-Blacks, and being so greatly privileged they will be supporters of the status quo such as you cannot ever hope to find anywhere. That is the new strategy of the Nationalist Government. The bitter pill is very significantly coated with sugar. Those who will belong to this core economy and society will be numerically insignificant, and will pose hardly any threat to the power-wielding White group. But what of the rest – the hapless *hoi polloi*? They will be, and are being, relegated to the outer darkness, the limbo of the forgotten. They must get out. The Riekert Commission has recommended, and it is a recommendation accepted with some alacrity, that "illegals", those who don't qualify, must be endorsed out on pain of an R500 maximum fine for those who should want to employ them.

Nobody repudiated Dr Mulder when he pointed out in Parliament that the logical conclusion of apartheid was that there would be no Black South Africans.

And to get to that conclusion, they have with very little compunction moved nearly two million Blacks. They have moved them often from places where they had reasonably adequate housing, where they were able to work – some in the informal sector, as casual labourers, within walking or reasonable distance of their places of work. They have moved them, dumped them as if they were potatoes, in largely inhospitable areas, often with no alternative accommodation. (The Makgatho people were moved just before Christmas 1974, a family feast in Christian South Africa, from their perfectly satisfactory homes to their new homes in tents. Even if it was absolutely vital that these people should be moved, why just before Christmas, and making it almost impossible for the children to write their year-end examinations?) They have increased transport costs: whereas before the Makgatho people were only 50km from Pietersburg, now they are 100km. From being daily commuters they have become weekend commuters. In Glenmore, an old man told me that in his old home he paid little for his fare to go and do some gardening in town. Now he would have to stay in town until Friday, otherwise his take-home pay would be whittled away to nothing. The people of Walmer, near Port Elizabeth, walk just across the railway line to find work in Walmer Town. Nobody wants them to move – the inhabitants of Walmer don't, and they themselves don't want to move. But they must be moved to Zwide, several kilometres from the town. They will have to pay a bus fare. They will have to swell a 12,000 waiting list for houses by another 6000. Why?

People are starving in most of these resettlement camps. I know, for I have seen it. They are starving not because of an accident or a misfortune. No, they are starving because of deliberate Government policy made in the name of White Christian civilization. They are starving; a little girl can tell you that when they can't borrow food, they drink water to fill their stomachs. This is the solution the Nationalists have decided upon. Many can't work, not because they won't work but because there is no work available. So they sit listlessly whilst we reap the benefits of a soaring gold price and our boom, which makes us want to import skilled labour from overseas. They are there as a reservoir, deliberately created, of cheap labour. When Black labour was needed, the laws forced Blacks into town when they were often well-to-do farmers. They had to become wage earners in order to pay the taxes levied on them. Now they are not really wanted, so they are endorsed out. There are probably two million Blacks unemployed and another million likely to lose their jobs, but they are out of sight and so are out of mind.

They are being made the responsibility willy-nilly of Bantustan governments that have no resources to cope with such a massive problem. Black poverty and Black unemployment, which are urban problems and have a fair chance of being solved in the urban setting, are transferred to the Bantustans which Dr Nash has called ghettoes of poverty, where there is no hope at all that they can be solved. The menfolk must perforce become migrant labourers. The women, the young and the aged must try to eke out an existence of sorts, with little hope of keeping body and soul together. Never mind what even the White Dutch Reformed Church has said in condemning the migratory labour system. That is the solution, the final stage of apartheid.

I wrote to the PM about what I could only call a diabolical policy – this policy of Black uprooting. I got back a courteous letter, and basically he was saying the removals are legal. Here in South Africa we tend to think that legal and morally right mean the same thing.

The cost

The cost in terms of human suffering is incalculable. Undernourishment, starvation and malnutrition have serious consequences in growing children. They may suffer irreversible brain damage, we are told. The *Financial Mail* last Friday had an article entitled "False Economy of Malnutrition" in which it says, "No one can calculate the cost of a generation growing up physically and mentally stunted . . . humanitarian considerations apart, the present neglect is false economy which costs the country millions of rand annually in hospitalization . . .

"The underlying cause – poverty, unemployment, the migrant labour system, ignorance and the overcrowded underdeveloped homelands – will take many years to eradicate . . . But these by-products of apartheid will remain a national responsibility" (*Financial Mail*, 21 March). And yet it is that very responsibility which the Government wants to shuffle off on to the Bantustans, which are too ill-equipped to deal with the problems.

Dr Nash points out the psychological effects of the trauma experienced as a result of any uprooting, most of all enforced removal. What is the cost to human beings reduced to such total despair that they can say, as they sit listlessly, with nothing to do although they are able-bodied, "We live only to die"?

But how do we compute the cost in the legacy of bitterness, anger, frustration and indeed hatred which we are leaving behind for our children? In the body of this paper I have described many things that have happened to us Blacks in this country during the several decades of our oppression and exploitation and deprivation. It is, I believe, a miracle of God's grace that Blacks still talk to Whites, to any Whites. It is a miracle of God's grace that Blacks still say that we want a non-racial South Africa for all of us, Black and White together. It is a miracle of God's grace that Blacks can still say they are committed to a ministry of justice and reconciliation and that they want to avert the bloodbath which seems more and more inevitable as we see little bending and give on the crucial issue of power-sharing. We are told that the Afrikaners have found it very difficult to forgive, certainly difficult to forget what the British did to them in the concentration camps. I want to say that Blacks are going to find it difficult, very difficult, to forgive, certainly difficult to forget what Whites have done and are doing to us in this matter of population removals.

All Blacks live in a constant state of uncertainty. Even I, a bishop in the Church of God and General Secretary of the South African Council of Churches, have no security. The township manager could in his wisdom decide that my continued presence in Soweto was detrimental to its good ordering and peace, and by the stroke of his pen would withdraw my permission to reside there, just like that. We each have such a sword of Damocles hanging over our heads. I don't suppose many Whites know this or, if they do, care too much about it.

The *Rand Daily Mail*, in a short editorial on 20 March 1980, on the Group Areas Act, under whose provisions much uprooting has taken place, referred to the statistics showing that 11,256 families had so far been moved. These statistics meant about 560,000 men, women and children had so far been uprooted. There were 23,022 families still to be moved, and the editorial notes: "This is human disruption on a staggering scale. Yet despite the Cillie Commission's finding about the resentment caused by this Act, it remains. Why?" And we echo, Why?

What the Church can do
The solutions are both long-term and short-term. The short-term strategy is to oppose all removals. We suggest that representations are made to the authorities to persuade them to desist forthwith. If we know about any removals likely to happen then let us do all we can to oppose them. If all our efforts to dissuade the authorities fail, then we should be there, physically present as the witnessing and caring Church. We must use all non-violent methods to hinder the act of demolition.

We should support those in resettlement camps, providing them with as much relief that they will need as possible – food, blankets, etc. And the Church should help to rehabilitate these shocked persons by being a serving Church, helping to develop a community spirit and helping the people help themselves. These are not empty phrases – the Crossroads people showed considerable ability until some of them were subverted by money.

No doubt population removals and the uprooting of people should be a priority concern, for it is a part of the

Total Strategy. The Church is being fragmented through the implementation of the Bantustan policy. This policy has very serious theological implications about the unity and integrity of the Church. How can a church minister faithfully or serve if it is constantly threatened with disabilities if it does not toe a specific political line? The so-called urban church is involved – the expense of rebuilding church structures and church congregations is quite staggering, and the Church is being torn asunder. "If one part of the body suffers, then the whole suffers with it . . ."

In the long term, the solution must be political. There are not two ways about it. Either there is going to be power-sharing or there is not. If not, then we must give up hope of a peaceful settlement in South Africa. If the Government is determined to go ahead with its Balkanization of South Africa on ethnic lines, and depriving Blacks of their South African citizenship, then we have had it, the ghastly alternative will be upon us. Population removals must stop immediately if we are to be able to work for a new kind of South Africa, and the Church should be in the forefront to prepare all of us for this new South Africa.

There is still a chance, but if we let it slip then it will be gone for ever. Neither the most sophisticated arsenal nor the best army or police force will give White South Africa true security, for that will come and come automatically when all of us, Black and White, know we count as of equal worth in the land of our birth, which we love with a passionate love. Please God, we pray you, let them hear us, let them hear us before it is too late.

White South Africa, please know that you are deluding yourselves, or you are allowing yourselves to be deluded, if you think that the present ordering of our society can continue. Blacks will be free whatever you do or don't do. That is not in question. Don't let the *when* and the *how* be in doubt. Don't delay our freedom, which is your freedom as well, for freedom is indivisible. Let it be now, and let it be reasonably peaceful. As I did to the students at Wits, so I call on all Whites to join the liberation struggle on God's side for justice, peace, righteousness, love, joy, laughter, compassion, caring and reconciliation.

This is the vision that upholds me:

After this I looked, and there was an enormous crowd – no one could count all the people! They were from every race, tribe, nation, and language, and they stood in front of the throne and of the Lamb, dressed in white robes and holding palm branches in their hands. They called out in a loud voice: "Salvation comes from our God, who sits on the throne, and from the Lamb!" All the angels stood round the throne, the elders, and the four living creatures. Then they threw themselves face downwards in front of the throne and worshipped God, saying, "Amen! Praise, glory, wisdom, thanksgiving, honour, power, and might belong to our God for ever and ever! Amen!" (Revelation 7:9–12; Good News Bible)

May it come true for our land.

Diakonia, Durban
March 1980

Black South African Perspectives
and the Reagan Administration

One rule about South Africa that has the validity of a Euclidian axiom is the one stating that on any major matter you can be sure that most White South Africans will be ranged on one side and the majority of Black South Africans will be found on the opposite one. Most White South Africans will, for instance, talk about terrorists and approve of any action to curb these bloodthirsty subversives, whereas most Blacks will refer to the self-same class of people as freedom fighters or at the least as guerrillas or insurgents. Possessing this rule about South Africa I have made you all instant experts on my beloved country.

Following the application of this rule, Blacks knew they were in trouble when their White compatriots went into transports of ecstatic delight and joy when Mr Ronald Reagan won the US Presidential elections. Anything that pleases most White South Africans cannot fail to depress most Blacks. But were Blacks justified in feeling so low that they could have crawled under a snake? The purpose of this paper is to expose the feelings of Black South Africans *vis-à-vis* the Reagan administration and to demonstrate that those feelings are not without reason.

We knew we were in real trouble from the start. A conference had been called in Geneva to be the precursor of the countdown to Namibian independence. I am not a politician, though there may be those who want to accuse me of being a politician trying very hard to be a bishop. My disclaimer is merely to point to my naïveté and lack of information which could be used to excuse any mistaken analysis I should make. With that proviso, I believe I am right when I declare that most right-thinking people and astute observers of the international scene were optimistic about the outcome of the Geneva Conference on Namibia and the so-called pre-implementation talks. Nearly everybody believed that there were only a few kinks to be ironed out and that the United Nations Transitional Assistance Group (UNTAG) would be in Namibia very shortly after that January conference. Nearly everybody was shocked when the internal parties, obviously acting as a front for the South Africans, presented quite substantial objections to the proposals in Geneva. The South Africans had read *their* signals correctly. They had surmised that a change of incumbent at the White House was going to lead to a policy of appeasement with the perpetrators of what Blacks believe to be the most vicious system since Nazism. And so South Africa and her surrogates became intransigent and raised difficulties which nobody had thought could be made to stand between the Conference and a Namibian settlement that would win the approval of the world. The South Africans scuppered the Geneva talks because they believed they were on to a good thing, a very good thing, with the advent of President Reagan to the White House. And they were right. It was the beginning of a series of shocks to Black expectations and aspirations. Can you imagine, it is Black children, who are actually like American children, who are having to go into exile and who are dying in the so-called operational area while South Africa, aided and abetted by the leader of the so-called free world, can score debating points about the impartiality or lack of it in the United Nations. It would be amusing, if it did not have such momentous and tragic consequences, to note that South Africa's hesitancy about free elections, etc., in Namibia is because they say categorically that they do not want a Marxist government in that country. Then how are the elections supposed to be free if South Africa wants to decide for the Namibians what would be good for them! It is exactly in line with her definition of self-determination internally in the Republic of South Africa. The Botha Government wins itself international plaudits by its declaration in favour of self-determination. This is admired universally, like motherhood, until you discover that the South African Government has pre-empted any real self-determination because it has decided that you can have self-determination as long as it is along ethnic lines within the framework of apartheid. But enough of that digression.

Constructive engagement

Reagan's people argued plausibly that President Carter had hardly succeeded in bringing home the bacon in his efforts to apply pressure on South Africa to improve her dismal record on human rights. It was argued that pressure merely made the Afrikaners and most White South Africans mad, and hardened them against all persuasion to ease the lot of Blacks or to apply some lubrication to the creaking joints of a political system that had gained universal opprobrium from the rest of the world as a system of injustice, exploitation and oppression. The White South Africans retreated into their *laager*, and contended that all that President Carter and his loquacious UN Ambassador Andy Young had succeeded in doing was to salve their consciences by striking moral poses – and perhaps to ingratiate themselves with the Third World and particularly Africa. Apart from this they had emerged totally empty-handed from their engagement with the South Africans. Such pressure, the Reaganites argued, clearly did not work, could not work, just as with economic pressure or sanctions. These had not worked to bring down Ian Smith. That had been accomplished by enlisting the support of

South Africa to lean on Smithie to persuade him to become a little more amenable to reason. The Carter strategy was largely empty rhetoric which revealed a poor grasp of the geo-political realities of the southern African situation.

All reasonable people would want to say that if one line of attack fails, then it is perfectly reasonable to make an assessment of that strategy and to try a different tack. So there was little wrong theoretically in the attitude of the new US administration. They wanted to see movement especially on the Namibian issue. They reaffirmed their adherence to UN Resolution 435. But they knew that there was not a snowball's chance in hell of its implementation without South Africa's collaboration. In their policy review (I suppose this has now been completed – though when I visited the US last year I was intrigued that quite a few people who held key positions regarding the African continent had in fact never even been to Africa, and confessed that their knowledge of the facts of the situation was somewhat minimal – has this changed?) they were determined to send clear signals to South Africa that relations between the two countries were in for a thaw. There was going to be a soft pedalling of public expressions of US indignation at South Africa's blatant violations of human rights. For an administration that had got significant support from the New Moral Right it was odd how it should be embarrassed with striking moral poses, and so concern for human rights was to be downgraded in the priorities that Mr Reagan set himself. America would not set itself up as the universal policeman any longer.

In fact, not only has the Reagan administration refrained by and large from rebuking South Africa for her violations of human rights, but it has actually found many occasions when it positively commended South Africa for things which we Blacks must say we found difficult to see as commendable at all. Early on in his first year as President, Mr Reagan actually was able to say that the US should not turn its back on South Africa and abandon an old friend who had fought side by side with the US in many of its wars, when South Africa need not have involved herself at all in all of this mayhem. He has recently repeated this extraordinary statement. Blacks have not only been surprised but completely bamboozled. Somebody needs lessons in elementary history, for surely nearly everybody ought to know that certainly in World War II many Afrikaners were opposed to fighting what they considered the Englishmen's war. Indeed Mr B. J. Vorster, sometime Prime Minister and State President, and his confidant, General van der Bergh, former head of what was styled the Bureau for State Security (BOSS), were both interned during that war because of their pro-Nazi sympathies. The White DRC used to drum out anyone who came to its services wearing the Defence Force uniform. Whilst the Afrikaner especially hoped for a Nazi victory, Black South Africans were supposed to face the might of Rommel's Afrika Korps armed only with a spear, because even under General Smuts South Africa was still a rigidly segregated society. Black men risked their lives (in World War I many Black lives were lost when the ship *Mendi* went down in the English Channel), largely because they had been promised a new kind of society in the land of their birth after the war. They were told they were fighting for freedom and liberation. It is galling in the extreme that those who tried to subvert the war effort should now be welcomed with open arms, whilst the descendants of those who were ready to make the supreme sacrifice should be discarded so shabbily.

Mr Reagan obviously is concerned about Soviet expansionism, and almost everything else is subordinated in his foreign policy to this almost obsessional concern to stem the tide of Communism. Any Government, however repressive, which declares itself opposed to Communism and the alleged Soviet desire for global hegemony becomes a blue-eyed boy of the Washington administration. It therefore was certainly no accident that the very first head of state to be welcomed by President Reagan after his inauguration should have headed the ghastly and repressive regime of South Korea, where many Christian leaders amongst others are languishing in gaol for opposing the totalitarian rule of their overlords. This is described as enlightened self-interest, but the victims of injustice and oppression all over the world are appalled when the leader of the free world gives respectability and the stamp of approval to those who are perpetrators of some of the most vicious systems in the world. It seems almost bizarre that a country founded on the principles of justice and freedom (when the thirteen Colonies found it intolerable to be subject to imperialist Britain) should so often be found hobnobbing with the world's most unfree governments. It is quite incredible that the US should be able to prop up regimes that are so repressive and unjust that those who have been killed to maintain these governments in power cry out to heaven to be avenged. The stink of their corpses is an affront to decency, and in the minds of simpletons it is all possible because of US support for the strangulation of freedom in their several countries. Just look at what is happening in El Salvador and other parts of Latin America. Isn't the price of enlightened self-interest in fact too high to pay for the alienation of the indigenous peoples of these lands, which are groaning under the yoke of corrupt and vicious men aided and abetted by the most powerful nation in the West? The US record in the matter of upholding human rights and justice in other lands is abysmal – what a paradox! It seems to me that self-interest, whether it be that of a nation or an individual, is ultimately self-stultifying, as Our Lord indicated it would be. We are talking after all of those who make great play of their Christianity and not about pagans.

South Africa realized quite quickly that she was on to a

good thing when she declared herself firmly and with alacrity as the last bastion of Western Christian civilization, a bulwark against the almost inexorable advance of predatory Communism. She had a Suppression of Communism Act on her statute book before you could say "Joe McCarthy". Foreigners did not stop to check on the definition of Communism contained in this piece of legislation, nor did they become sceptical when its provisions were being used against committed Christians who just happened to be implacable opponents of apartheid. No, it was enough that there was this pugnacious ally who would keep the sea lanes free of Soviet influence. Similarly the South African Government's insistence on the use of the term "terrorist" to apply to those whom others designate "freedom fighter" or at least "insurgent" is not merely accidental. The free world is plagued by terrorists, in Ulster, in West Germany, in Italy especially, and it is fed up with those whom it considers lawless louts. They do not stop to consider the difference between those who have legitimate channels for expressing their views which they refuse to use, and those who have hardly any such means. And so the US is intent on retaining South Africa as an ally, despite the cost to its own credibility in the eyes of the Third World at not distancing itself from the international pariah for her obnoxious racial policy.

It is strange that so far this attempted *rapprochement* does not seem to have brought home the bacon either. But more of that later. The USA wants to get the Cubans out of Angola, perceiving them as Soviet surrogates. Now the problems of southern Africa have not been more clearly demonstrated as interlocking than by the whole issue of the Cuban presence in Angola. Unless the Namibian question is settled, the Angolans will continue to give bases to the South West Africa People's Organization (SWAPO) which South Africa will continue to bombard by her incursions into Angola. The Angolans are unable single-handedly to cope with the

terrifying military might of South Africa, which she has
obtained thanks to a compliant and conniving Western bloc
of nations which helped South Africa to arm to the teeth.
Angola therefore will have to keep the Cubans as her ultimate
line of defence against the rampant South Africans.
Consequently, by not getting South Africa to deal more
expeditiously with the Namibian issue the US is in fact
subverting its own intentions to see the Soviet surrogate out
of the African sub-continent.

The US has signalled the dramatic change in its attitude
to South Africa since the advent of President Reagan in other
ways which have left us Blacks aghast. There was the clumsy
incident of those military men who visited Washington and
the interesting Mrs Jean Kirkpatrick. There has been the
increase in consuls and in military attachés, and the refusal
even to consider the application of economic pressure on
South Africa as being totally counter-productive, etc; we
shall have to come back to this intriguing subject anon.
There has been the alacrity with which the US, usually
accompanied by other Western countries, has been willing
to come to South Africa's assistance in warding off the
application of mandatory UN sanctions through the exercise
of their veto power, protecting what the victims of the system
see as the perpetrators of injustice and oppression on a scale
unprecedented in any country that claims to belong to the
Western family of nations. We have noted the reluctance
with which the Reagan administration issues condemnatory
statements (so that we were somewhat pleasantly taken aback
at the statement from the State Department criticizing the
confiscation of my passport for the second time) against
blatant examples of South African injustice and oppression,
e.g. the callous treatment of the Nyanga squatters or the
spate of bannings and detentions without trial. Instead we
have been shocked at the almost indecent alacrity with which
the Reagan administration has pronounced on what it

perceived to be changes in the right direction on the part of the Botha regime. The US has spoken with strange enthusiasm about the rhetoric for reform, which in hardly any instance has been translated into concrete reality. The psychology of this approach is quite admirable. Use as much carrot as possible to urge the reluctant creature forward. You are more likely to succeed than if you resort to the heavy-handed belabouring with a stick. And perhaps if this different strategy had been proving successful, Blacks in South Africa might just have been persuaded to become some sort of masochists and enjoy the pain because of its efficacious consequences in dismantling apartheid. The US under President Reagan would then be justified in running the gauntlet of international disapproval in the short term, because it could then gloat in the end since it had accomplished what had eluded his predecessor.

Has this strategy shown positive results?
I am no expert on these things, but from my perspective I should be able to say without fear of contradiction and categorically that at this point in time (to use a phrase made notorious at a certain period in US contemporary history) this strategy has failed. A priority for the West and so for the US has been to find an acceptable solution for Namibia. We were much closer to a solution at the time of the abortive Geneva talks than we seem to be now. Instead of South Africa and her surrogates in the internal parties trying to be amenable to international efforts to secure a just settlement and growing in reasonableness, the opposite appears to be the case. They have increased their intransigence and their susceptibilities. They are becoming past masters at finding elements in the proposals to which to take exception. They say that SWAPO is totally unrepresentative. Now this may be true, but if they believe their own assertions, then they ought not to be afraid of going to the polls, because they

would be assured of an election victory. Their present strategy seems to betray the true position, that they are apprehensive of a SWAPO victory *à la* Mugabe in Zimbabwe, and it appears they want to delay the inevitable for as long as possible in the hope of bringing about enough reforms in the territory to give the internal parties the ghost of a chance in the election contest. They refuse to realize that in the eyes of the people, to be friendly with South Africa is to be friendly with the oppressor, is to collaborate with those who have allegedly perpetrated unspeakable atrocities in the north of Namibia. Should the internal parties ever win, then we Blacks in South Africa will know that it was almost certainly a rigged election and Namibia would still have to be liberated, since South Africa would have succeeded in installing puppets whose strings were being pulled in Pretoria. The South African Government shudders at the prospects of a SWAPO administration in Windhoek. They fear the internal repercussions in South Africa; raising, as did the liberation of Mozambique, Angola and Zimbabwe, Black expectations for their own freedom, and strengthening the presssure from the so-called right which would exploit what it saw as a selling out of the Whites in Namibia. So they are taking exception at every conceivable point, knowing rightly that President Reagan and his band will continue to back them. In the meantime, as I said at the beginning, our children and their parents in Namibia must bear the brunt of the war caused by racists.

Even should an acceptable solution be arrived at, we Blacks will hardly praise the five for this. It was delayed those several years since the Geneva talks, when it should have happened and would almost certainly have happened had it not been for the fact that the Americans chose to put Mr Reagan in the White House. A Namibian solution would be no more than they should have achieved, and little thanks would be due to them. They will not bring back to life those who have been killed so needlessly, and so why should we thank them when they are encouraging South Africa to engage in superfluous debating contests?

Constructive engagement might be worthwhile, for instance, if it meant that it gave the US great influence over South Africa to persuade her to take one line of action rather than another. But this does not seem to be the case with Angola either. Instead of being able to restrain South Africa from violating the territory of a sovereign country, the opposite has seemed to happen. South Africa has with impunity made audacious incursions into Angola. An EEC investigation speaks of as many as 2000 such forays. In South Africa there is considerable censorship of news relating to military matters. The outside world knows more about such things, and we South Africans get to know only what the authorities deem fit to release, and of course they are all honourable men releasing untampered news without bias! We know that certain overseas media have been able to report some hair-raising accounts of atrocities committed against the civilian Angolan population as well as against genuine refugees, action which will tend to be described in South Africa as engagement with SWAPO's "terrorists". Even Dr Savimbi, who appears to have the Reagan administration's nod of approval, recently condemned South Africa, but she goes on regardless because she falls under the protective umbrella of the US Government, which shields her from international disapprobation. Without this she would not behave in such a manner – showing scant regard for what the rest of the world thinks. We place the blame for this disgraceful conduct firmly and squarely on the shoulders of the US Government. It will have an awful lot to answer for in the world's tribunals one day, when we can arraign it for really being unbelievably an enemy of human freedom.

Perhaps something positive could be said for constructive engagement if we could show that internally things were moving towards change in South Africa. I am afraid that the search in this area will prove equally as fruitless as in the other areas that we have examined. No doubt there has been much encouraging rhetoric. Mr P. W. Botha has called to the Whites to "adapt or die"; Dr Koornhof has repeatedly declared that he was fighting the much-hated Pass Laws which control the every movement of Blacks. He declared in the US some time ago that apartheid was dead but sadly we have not seen the corpse and we have not been invited to the funeral. There have been commendable advances in labour legislation, notably the recognition accorded to Black labour unions. Unfortunately these gains have been largely nullified by the harassment, detention without trial and bannings to which the leaders of the unions have been subjected in order to emasculate the organizations and render them ineffective. No, apartheid is as alive as ever, if not more so. There are now four so-called independent Bantustans designed to turn Blacks into aliens in their own land. This is apartheid's final solution, as the extermination of the Jews was Nazism's. Nearly two million Blacks have been callously uprooted from their original homes and dumped, as you dump rubbish, in the Bantustans, where they must starve because there is no work and little land for cultivation. A few Blacks in the urban areas are gaining substantial concessions in the form of better jobs, better wages. The aim is to create a middle class to act as a buffer between the largely affluent Whites and the vast majority of Blacks, who must languish in the outer darkness of rural poverty and starvation. Some cosmetic improvements have been effected but apartheid's unjust structures remain as entrenched as ever they were. As Mrs Sally Motlana, Vice President of the SACC has said, "We don't want our chains made comfortable. We want them removed."

Detention without trial continues. Detainees are held under the notorious Section 6 of the Terrorism Act and remain incommunicado at the pleasure of the police. To date forty-six people have died in detention. Most famous of these persons is Steve Biko. As I write, the first White person to die in detention, Dr Neil Aggett, was found allegedly hanged in his cell. Those detained include labour union and church leaders and students without benefit of habeas corpus.

Bannings are continuing unabated. Mrs Winnie Mandela, wife of Nelson Mandela imprisoned on Robben Island for life, had her five-year banning order renewed for a further five years when it expired last December. I don't recall that the US protested this arbitrary act of turning a human being into a non-person.

I am unable to see what the US has to show as a positive gain from South Africa for its policy of constructive engagement. It seems to me that the giving or the bending backwards have all been on the side of the US. Dr Chester Crocker, the Assistant Secretary of State for African Affairs, made an extraordinary statement all in line with the new Reagan policy towards South Africa. He said that in the struggle between Black and White in South Africa, the US would not take sides. Admirable impartiality, but how can you be impartial in a situation of injustice and oppression? To be impartial and not to take sides, is indeed to have taken sides already. It is to have sided with the status quo. It is small comfort to a mouse, if an elephant is standing on its tail, to say, "I am impartial." In this instance, you are really supporting the elephant in its cruelty. How are you to remain impartial when the South African authorities evict helpless mothers and children and let them shiver in the winter rain, as even their flimsy plastic covers are destroyed? This action brought tears to some US Congress people when they witnessed this cruelty.

Recently two commissions of inquiry have reported: one is the Steyn Commission on the Media, which would tighten the screws on the press and hamper the relatively free flow of information: and the other is the Rabie Commission, which wants to tighten the already draconian security legislation, including detention without trial and banning, which they justify as necessary in these critical days. The US is determined to have such friends.

Black reaction

We have been deeply hurt. We have seen that when it comes to the matter of Black freedom then we Blacks are really expendable in the view of the mighty US. It was a case of blood being thicker than water. You can't really trust Whites. When it comes to the crunch, whatever the morality involved, Whites will stick by their fellow Whites. At least under the Carter administration our morale was upheld by their encouraging rhetoric of disapproval. They did not, as is happening now, lend respectability to a horrible system. They seemed to care about our plight. They did not talk about the overriding strategic importance of South Africa, with her wealth in key strategic resources which were to be more important than human freedom. South African Blacks during the Carter administration by and large held the US in high regard. Its embassy staff were among the few Whites who were welcomed to such highly emotional occasions as commemorations of 16 June. I would hazard a guess that it would be as much as their lives are worth for the same personnel to risk attending such gatherings now. I suspect that they would be drummed out unceremoniously. I am personally fond of most of these people, but as my own personal little protest at the actions of the Reagan administration I no longer attend US embassy functions nor do I see Reagan administration people. I made an exception last December to see USAID people and I told them so. I let them know my very deep feelings on these matters.

We asked, and continue to ask, the international community to apply political, diplomatic but above all economic

116

pressure on the South African authorities to persuade them to come to the conference table to work out a solution for our crisis before it is too late. It is our only chance of a reasonably peaceful solution. For advocating this I have lost my passport for a second time. Constructive engagement can't get even that returned.

The US Government gave us an eloquent spiel on the general ineffectiveness of sanctions, that they had to be applied by several countries at the same time, etc. etc. There might have been merit in these observations, but they lost all credibility for us. Why? Well, when the Polish Government applied martial law in Poland, who applied sanctions, and unilaterally at that? Why, it was the self-same US that can't see its way to doing half of what it did against the Polish Government and the Russians. The US Government does not really care about Blacks. Poles are different. They are White.

Our people are rapidly despairing of a peaceful resolution in South Africa. Those of us who still speak "peace" and "reconciliation" belong to a rapidly diminishing minority. And if they decide to fight, they know they can't go to the West for support. So we are paradoxically being driven into the arms of the Soviets to get our arms, by the very country that is concerned about Soviet expansionism.

Freedom is coming. We will be free whatever anybody does or does not do about it. We are concerned only about *how* and *when*. It should be soon, and we want it to be reasonably peaceful. When we are free South Africa will still be of strategic importance and her natural resources will still be of strategic significance and we will remember who helped us to get free. The Reagan administration is certainly not on that list. Will your CIA now be out to get me?

Taped message to the Trans Africa Forum in the US
February 1982

The Role of White Opposition in South Africa

Introduction

The title as it stands is somewhat ambiguous. Are we meant to discuss the whole gamut of White opposition to the establishment, or are we expected to deal only with the Parliamentary Opposition? The former interpretation would mean that we had to examine the role of so-called right-wing opposition to the Nationalists, such phenomena as the Wit Kommando, the Kappie Kommando, the Aksie Eie Toekoms and the Herstigte Nazionale Party (HNP) as well. But it would also mean dealing with the role of White bodies such as the Black Sash, with its quite outstanding record of protest and opposition to current policies.

Since this is an article for a PFP (Parliamentary Federal Party) periodical I am inclined to veer towards the second interpretation – of Opposition with a capital "O" as referring to the official Opposition in the Westminster type of parliamentary democracy which we appear to enjoy in South Africa. I have said "appear" advisedly, because those who condemn the PFP for continuing in Parliament do so precisely on the grounds that they merely help to foster the illusion that South Africa has at least the trappings of a democracy, the façade of a duly and democratically elected Government and its equally democratically and duly elected Opposition. This enables the Government, so the critics continue, to claim that South Africa is not like the Latin

American banana republics or the military regimes of Africa and other parts of the Third World, and she can justly claim to belong to the Western world which sets high store, so it is averred, by democratic institutions. But more of that later.

It will be more manageable to deal with the subject as referring primarily to the Opposition rather than to opposition. In any case I do not think we could really regard the so-called right wing as an opposition, because their aim is not the dismantling of apartheid and the creation of a new kind of society in the Republic of South Africa, one in which race and colour would be seen to be just as ridiculous and irrelevant for judging the worth of a person as, for instance, the size of one's nose or the colour of one's eyes. Imagine a country where qualification to enter a university were to be determined by whether one had a large nose or not, and if you did not possess such a proboscis then you had to obtain a special permit to enter this institution of higher learning reserved for those with large noses.

No, a true Opposition would be one that offered a radical alternative to the bankrupt and barren policies of our current rulers, and which realized that the hope for this beautiful land lay in pursuing policies which upheld the dignity of persons just because they were human persons and, from the Judaeo-Christian perspective from which I write, were persons of infinite value because they were created in the image of the triune God. Their value was intrinsic to who they were and did not depend on merely extraneous biological factors over which they had no ultimate control. It depended not on whether they were or were not voracious consumers or producers, but simply and solely on the fact that God had created them and that He endowed them with inalienable rights such as the right to security from poverty and disease, the right to freedom of association, the right to work and to a decent family life, freedom of thought and

119

worship and movement. The so-called right wing merely seeks to extend and intensify the application of apartheid and so they should be seen as the pawns of the apartheid merchants – the Nationalists. After all, it was these self-same Nationalists who in order to gain political power in 1948 used the reprehensible *swartgevaar* tactics, "Do you want your daughter to marry this man?", showing a picture of a dishevelled and unkempt Black, and expecting the answer they got, a resounding "No", which sent them into Parliament as the winners of the electoral contest. As an irrelevant aside, Blacks nowadays retort to such despicable methods, "Let's see your daughter first!"

It was the Nats (Nationalists) who described in gory detail the horrendous consequences of what would have been no more than racial justice, allowing people to choose where they could live, whom they would want to marry, where they could work, etc. They went on an orgy of separating this, that and the other, building separate entrances and exits here, there and everywhere, being utterly wasteful of human resources in their obsession with *herrenvolkism*, duplicating facilities unequally with gay and wantonly wasteful abandon, and the country is only now coming a cropper because of all these misguided policies. The HNP and those of that lunatic fringe are merely people who have taken the Nats at their word and won't believe them when they say the opposite of what they had been preaching for so long. The HNP and the others are what a Nat will evolve into when their policies are taken to their logical conclusion. So we can discount them as an opposition. They are something of purists, and accuse the Nationalist Government of being deviationists. Perhaps behind the Iron Curtain there would have been a purge with considerable bloodletting, though we must not underestimate the animosity and other sordid emotions that were released over the Info Scandal, leading to the unprecedented resignations of a State President and a

Cabinet Minister who came within a whisker of being Prime Minister.

And we must not go on believing the whole business of Mr P. W. Botha's being hamstrung by his fears of the right wing. Mr Vorster had a parliamentary majority unlike any held by any of his predecessors, and he had swept the floor with the self-same HNP, and yet he too was paralysed. On those occasions, to excuse his lack of action we were told it was because he was concerned for the unity of Afrikanerdom. The country was being held to ransom for this illusion. The last election has shown that there is no such thing as Afrikaner unity, and the Prime Minister should sing 'Hallelujah' for being set free of this albatross. He can never satisfy the right because every concession he makes to them merely increases their appetite. He should with his majority go decisively for radical reform, not a tinkering with the peripheral aspects of apartheid, trying cosmetically to turn a monster into a beauty. It can't be done.

A true Opposition

The Opposition has attempted to provide a radical alternative to apartheid and certainly has a vision of a non-racial South African society where human beings are valued for just that, where the rule of law holds sway so that the executive cannot rule by decree in an arbitrary manner and where habeas corpus has been restored. And so they have passed the first and most important test for being considered an Opposition. Their *raison d'être* is to dismantle the status quo and build a beautiful new tomorrow, where our security is assured because all have a stake and a place in the sun of such a South Africa.

I have questions about details in the PFP constitutional proposals, especially the veto granted to minorities, which seems a device to let in ethnicity by the back door, and we Blacks (most of us) execrate ethnicity with all our being.

121

Surely a bill of rights to protect *individual* rather than *group* rights would meet the point that this constitutional provision attempts to cover. But I don't want to split hairs, because on the whole I find these proposals largely acceptable. I certainly don't want to dominate anybody. I don't want to drive anybody into the sea. So the PFP is a legitimate Opposition in the proper sense. But does it have a viable role?

Role of the Opposition?

There are many radical youths, Black and White, who question the existence of the PFP as a Parliamentary Opposition. Their point is that South Africa is not a democracy in the accepted sense of that word, meaning that all adult persons have the vote and are eligible for public office. South Africa is a racial oligarchy, and by continuing to be in Parliament, especially with a small presence (albeit one that has grown), the PFP is helping to give the illusory impression that South Africa is in fact a parliamentary democracy, when all we have is the façade and the reality is non-existent.

We have a charade that takes place in Cape Town because there is little that the Government cannot bulldoze through Parliament, given their massive majority. And let the PFP not dismiss this stricture too lightly. Our rulers *are* past masters at providing the shadow for the substance and at playing games. For instance, they are glad to confound their overseas critics by maintaining a relatively free press, which seen against the backdrop of what happens elsewhere on the African continent seems to put South Africa in the Western camp. We should not argue at the moment about the considerable constraints placed on the media and their own somewhat lily-livered self-censorship. We do have a relatively free press, and it is an anomaly that sticks out like a sore thumb in the general repressive atmosphere of our land. Our rulers will pass laws against Communism, and speak about terrorists, about free enterprise, so that overseas people would want to say that South Africa shares their value system. And when you add that there *is* an Opposition in Parliament then the propaganda war is being won. I think the PFP have on one occasion walked out of Parliament because they had been accused of being lukewarm patriots or something of that nature. I suspect the Government were shocked by that manoeuvre. It could well be that, in the end, the most effective opposition gambit would be to walk out and stay out if it became clear the Government was immovable and totally intransigent.

I suppose the Opposition could argue that they have a positive role. First, they represent a significant dissenting sector of the White community, and in a country with hardly any tradition of dissent to speak about (with the notable exception of the incredible Black Sash), a great deal can be said just for articulating that voice of reason.

Then it could, secondly, be argued that they give voice to the views of those voiceless millions, the Black community, in trying to articulate as far as they can their aspirations, hopes and fears.

Thirdly, it is possible that despite the massive majority the Government enjoys, they are still held up even for a short while by the Parliamentary debate and can't ride too roughshod since they must give some sort of account in Parliament. They are often able to bypass Parliament by declaring that it is not in the public interest to divulge such and such, but even when they do this, I suppose they must feel a slight twinge of conscience, or are they long past it?

Fourthly, it has been the probing of the Opposition that has led to things such as the Info Scandal and its interesting repercussions, after the press had played its splendidly courageous role through investigative journalism. It can be argued that without the Opposition to goad it, the Government would have been quite happy to sit, knowing that there had been collusion between a Prime Minister and a senior Cabinet Minister, and be less than forthcoming in their dealings with the public and with Parliament.

Fifthly, there would have been no Helen Suzman. Can you imagine a more bleak and more desolate prospect?

Sixthly, we could say the PFP gives Blacks hope in so far as they can say that not all Whites are bad.

And yet the more cogent the arguments are for a real role for the Opposition, the more it could be said that they do give credibility to the system, that it is not so bad. It does allow for very considerable debate and argument, and that is something that makes the outside world think you need to have your head read when you say we are really qualified candidates, as a country, to be a police state, or as near this as really makes no difference. The victims of apartheid can't be bothered with academic niceties. They experience apartheid as a vicious system, totally evil without remainder, and they may one day condemn the PFP for having collaborated in their oppression, admittedly with the best will and intentions.

Conclusion
Actually the PFP is going to have to decide soon whether it is going to be part of the charade determined by the architects of apartheid or not.

I predicted last year that within five to ten years we will have a Black Prime Minister. One year has gone past. We don't have very much time left over. Will this happen reasonably peacefully or after much violence and bloodshed? This is the context in which the PFP and White opponents of apartheid have to decide.

South Africa – Some Crystal-gazing

Hope, so they say, springs eternal in the human breast. After all the buffetings that the Black community has taken from over thirty years of Nationalist apartheid rule, you would have thought the stuffing would be knocked out of the Blacks and that by now they would have become seasoned cynics. Mr Vorster had proclaimed that he wanted six months when he would transform the political face of South Africa. Mr Pik Botha, who was at the same time his Ambassador at the UN, had also declared with a great flourish that South Africa was moving away from discrimination based on race. And what had happened? Nothing more than the intransigence that had led to the uprisings of 16 June 1976 and the orgy of bannings and detentions without trial, capped by the death in detention of Steve Biko, a death which had left the then Minister of Justice and Police, Mr Jimmy Kruger, cold, as he had announced to a cheering Nationalist Party Congress.

Clearly nothing was about to change. The White oligarchy was determined to cling to power at all costs – that these costs included Black lives and Black freedom did not seem to cause many people too much insomnia. And yet when Mr P. W. Botha came on the scene, hopes began to run high again. Here was a man who appeared decisive, who knew that White South Africa must adapt or die. He was speaking in a way that we had not expected to hear from a Nationalist Prime Minister. He seemed to have set his sights on reform, and realized he would need new allies, hence his successful overtures to the private sector. He knew that the traditional supporters of his party would be appalled at having to give up so much of White privilege. A recent survey showed that 60 per cent of the Blacks thought Mr P. W. Botha was doing a good job as Prime Minister. That is how high hopes were flying.

The reality

It is nearly two years now, and there has been little more than reformist rhetoric which has not yet been translated into reality. There has been the "Info Scandal", which has kept rearing its ugly head. Mr Botha has made a valiant effort to streamline Government bureaucracy but he has also been concentrating power more and more in his own hands. He is increasingly seeking to bypass Parliament, as witness the abolition of the Senate and the new scheme for nominating parliamentarians. He has to be given credit for the advent of the President's Council, which represents revolutionary thinking on the part of the Nationalists, for up to this point it was taken as read that only Whites would decide the future of South Africa, constitutional or otherwise. The President's Council says other races (excluding Africans) will join the Whites in this exercise. Having got so far one asks in exasperation why, oh why, did he have to vitiate this potentially revolutionary move by two fatal flaws – the exclusion of the vast majority of this land and by having a nominated rather than an elected membership?

Even after this setback, many people hoped against hope that change, real fundamental change which has to do with political power-sharing, still might happen. So far we were being regaled with a diet of fine rhetoric and little else. Mr Botha, people were beginning to suspect, however, was going to be hoisted on the petard of Afrikaner unity, for like all his predecessors he did not want to have the dubious honour of going down in history as the man who split the

Nationalist Party and so also Afrikanerdom, never mind what happened to the country which would be held to ransom. The Prime Minister was humiliated by Dr Andries Treurnicht, the arch-conservative leader of the Transvaal Nationalist Party, on the question of Craven Week – whether school boys of different races could play rugby together during that week. Dr Treurnicht declared in public, contradicting the Prime Minister, that it would not happen. Mr Botha learned that if he took this momentous issue to the Party caucus he would lose to Dr Treurnicht, and so he backed down.

For various reasons, Mr Botha decided to call an election some two years before he need have done so. Perhaps he wanted his own mandate from the people and not Mr Vorster's. Perhaps he hoped to wipe the floor with the right wing and so be rid of them for ever. And he might have done both these things had he gone boldly for a reformist platform. Unfortunately, he retreated into the *laager* of well-tried traditional Afrikaner policies, and predictably this time he lost to both the right and the left. He was not conservative enough for the right and not reformist enough for the left (if these terms mean anything in South Africa). If he were bright he would realize that he has been relieved of the albatross of Afrikaner unity. It no longer exists.

Two options

I have spent time on Mr Botha because he holds the key to a peaceful future for South Africa. The point which is indisputable is that we who are oppressed will be free. That is not in question. The logic of history, even Afrikaner history, dictates that this is so. All that the Whites can do is to decide whether they want freedom to come reasonably peacefully or through bloodshed and the armed struggle. Those are the only options available. Mr Botha can play a decisive role by opting for a bold policy of change. Anything else will fail. He won't ever satisfy the right wing. So he should go all out to win the world and the rest of South Africa by opting for political power-sharing.

Apartheid, we were told by Dr Koornhof, is dead. Sadly we have not been invited to the funeral nor have we seen the corpse. Nothing short of moves towards dismantling apartheid will bring true security and peace to this land. Multi-national corporations with their Codes of Conduct are not yet involved in the business of helping to destroy apartheid. They have done some good things for their employees, but all within the framework of apartheid and really no more than what a good employer should have been doing. Ultimately their efforts are improvements not change. They are making apartheid more comfortable, rather than dismantling it. But, as Mrs Motlana said, "We don't want our chains made comfortable. We want them removed." They are investing in what I have called the most vicious system since Nazism, where 2,000,000 Blacks have been forcibly uprooted and dumped in the Bantustans – Bantustans which are ghettoes of poverty and misery as well as reservoirs of cheap Black migratory labour that play havoc with Black family life.

Unrest in the schools, on the labour front, is endemic in our country and will continue to be so until political power-sharing becomes a reality. More and more Blacks are becoming disillusioned as those of us calling for change by peaceful means have our credibility eroded by the action of the authorities, often brutal and excessive action. Calls for peaceful change are being answered by tear-gas, police dogs, bullets, detention without trial and banning orders. We are back in the dark ages of Mr Kruger. The authorities are growing in intransigence – belatedly Mr Botha wants to demonstrate that he is tough and cannot be trifled with.

He is too late because he has not come to terms with the determination, bordering on recklessness, of Black youth who flaunt ANC (African National Congress) emblems openly. He cannot control the militancy of Black labour unions which are going to be the power to watch.

There will be more and more police harassment, bannings and detentions, but these will not deter those who are determined to become free. The international community must make up its mind whether it wants to see a peaceful resolution of the South African crisis or not. If it does, then let it apply pressure (diplomatic, political but above all economic) on the South African Government to persuade them to go to the negotiating table with the authentic leaders of all sections of the South African population before it is too late. Maybe it is too late, judging from the conduct of the Reagan administration – then what Mr Vorster called "the alternative too ghastly to contemplate" is upon us. But hope springs eternal in the human breast.

Article written specially for African–American Institute
July 1981

CHAPTER 4

The Divine Intention

South Africa was recently described as a country whose political system has "no self-correcting mechanism capable of beginning the dismantlement of apartheid".* Bishop Tutu has warned elsewhere that a racial war in South Africa could possibly trigger off a global confrontation between the superpowers,† so the peaceful resolution of South Africa's political anomalies is an issue that goes far beyond its borders. How does Bishop Tutu see the will of God working in such a situation?

Chapter 4 opens with a moving tribute to Frikkie Conradie, an Afrikaner priest who went to serve the Black community in Alexandra Township near Johannesburg. His example, like the non-segregated worship in St Mary's Cathedral, Johannesburg, is a pointer to the divine intention for South Africa.

"What Jesus Means to Me" and "Love Reveals My Neighbour" are in different ways calls for self-respect, personal dignity, and compassionate action in the face of

* Basil Davidson, Canon Collins memorial lecture 1982.
† *Crying in the Wilderness*, Mowbray 1982, p. 109.

the apartheid system, and the sermon preached on the Feast for Epiphany stresses the importance of service to others.

"The Divine Intention" is the text of Bishop Tutu's testimony before an inquiry, the Eloff Commission, set up by the South African Government to investigate alleged financial irregularities within the South African Council of Churches (SACC). The aim of this was, as Bishop Tutu said, "totally unsubtle" – an attempt to discredit and render ineffective the assistance given by the SACC to the victims of apartheid. "The Divine Intention" is Bishop Tutu's defence of it, and a statement of the power of endurance of the Christian Church in the face of State persecution. – Ed.

The Funeral of Frikkie Conradie

When Our Lord died on the cross, we are told that the veil of the Temple was torn from top to bottom. For the Evangelists it represented the fact that God and us were reconciled.

Jesus cried out triumphantly, "It is finished – it is accomplished." What the Father had sent Me to do I have done – God and man have become friends again. And St Paul declared, "God was in Christ reconciling the world to Himself", and that we have been given the Gospel of reconciliation.

We have been made ambassadors of Christ to speak on behalf of God in Christ – to be reconciled with God.

If we are reconciled with God then we would be reconciled with one another.

We have come to thank God that He gave us such a wonderful gift as our dearly beloved Frikkie Conradie. The last time I saw him was Wednesday of last week, wearing that gentle smile that endeared him to so many people. If we want to sum up his life we should say that here was an ambassador of Christ, one who lived out a costly form of reconciliation. Can you imagine the unimaginable in this country of separation, of bitterness, of suspicion and hatred: can you imagine an Afrikaner, a DRC dominee of all people, leaving his own community to identify himself so closely with the downtrodden, the poor and the suffering, a White man giving himself and his family to a Black community, to be their servant and to work for justice and reconciliation and to work under a Black minister? It is unbelievable and yet we saw this miracle of God's grace working here in Alexandra Township, here in South Africa.

God be praised for Frikkie. Marietjie, thank you for sharing this wonderful man with us. You are a remarkable woman too, for you asked that he should be buried here with his people, his new people in Christ, to show most wonderfully that Christ has broken down the barriers between races, that in Christ we are all one.

Thank you God, thank you Marietjie, for giving us hope of the new society God is building in South Africa. He will strengthen you and your son, whom some people have called Vusumuzi – the one who raises up the house of Conradie. There will be a fulfilment of the vision in the book of Revelation.

After this I looked and saw a vast throng, which no one could count, from every nation, of all tribes, peoples and languages, standing in front of the throne and before the Lamb. They were robed in white and had palms in their hands, and they shouted together:

132

"Victory to our God who sits on the throne, and to the Lamb!" And all the angels stood round the throne and the elders and the four living creatures, and they fell on their faces before the throne and worshipped God, crying: "Amen! Praise and glory and wisdom, thanksgiving and honour, power and might, be to our God for ever and ever, Amen!" (Revelation 7:9–12; NEB)

Alexandra, Johannesburg
March 1982

St Mary's Cathedral, Johannesburg

In the early 1950s I used to come to the old Darragh House to be trained for the subdiaconate by Father Shand, SSJE. I liked going into the Cathedral to spend some quiet moments in the Holy Spirit Chapel, in front of the Blessed Sacrament. I cherished these moments as oases in the concrete wilderness of Johannesburg.

On other occasions when I popped into the Cathedral I would be fortunate to catch the boy choristers being rehearsed. You know how cherubic they always managed to look, as if butter could not melt in their mouths, and you knew that they could be up to all kinds of mischief. You forgot all that when you heard the dulcet tones coming over the air during those wonderful occasions when divine worship came from St Mary's.

So the two things I remember about the Cathedral are still

a wonderful part of its life. I refer to the extraordinary feature of people popping into the Cathedral either on their way to or from work to be quiet in the stillness of the darkened sanctuary. There is no question whatever that our Cathedral is thoroughly prayed in and by all kinds of people – Black people, White people, big people, little people, representatives of the variegated family of God find a warm welcome. It is a tremendous tradition. I have never known the Cathedral to be without at least one person with head bowed and lips moving, in silent thanksgiving or in anguished supplication like Hannah of old. You feel a little what the writer of Hebrews meant about the cloud of witnesses surrounding us – in the Cathedral you have a tremendous sense of belonging to a prayerful and devout fellowship.

The second feature that attracted me even in those early days was the music and the total liturgy. This surely must be as it should be – the Cathedral, the Mother Church of the diocese, where high standards are maintained in liturgy and music, a worthy offering to the triune majesty of God: Father, Son and Holy Spirit. Of course, since the Cathedral was/is also a parish church, a balance has had to be struck between elaborate and beautiful choral settings and congregational participation, and we will have to live with the tensions between these two aspects.

Speaking about the Cathedral as Mother Church brings me to a third feature discovered a little later, and that is how in a fragmented and race-mad society the Cathedral used to be the setting for really awesome and beautiful diocesan occasions, especially Synod Sunday. There just was nothing more compelling and impressive than when St Mary's was full to overflowing with all God's children of all races – with the long processions of catechists, subdeacons and clergy winding their way slowly into a Cathedral packed to the rafters. Hymns were sung in a babel of tongues, lessons read in another, and then we listened to the prophetic pronouncements of our father in God proclaiming the eternal Gospel of God's love for all His children, binding us all in a fellowship that transcended all irrelevant barriers and distinctions, telling of the will of God for the South Africa of that day. It was heady stuff – we were all together then though the policies of the politicians decreed that we be separated. What a great loss not to have a hall near the Cathedral in which to hold our Synods, because they were binding and healing occasions, our physical presence being a proclamation of our oneness in Our Lord and Saviour Jesus Christ.

And so it was exciting to follow in the footsteps of stalwarts such as Deans Palmer, Randolph and ffrench-Beytagh, and others who had established a scintillating tradition of worship, music, preaching and social witness. I will always have a lump in my throat when I think of the children at St Mary's, pointers to what can be if our society would but become sane and normal. Here were children of all races playing, praying, learning and even fighting together, almost uniquely in South Africa. And as I have knelt in the Dean's stall at the superb 9.30 High Mass, with incense, bells and everything, watching a multi-racial crowd file up to the altar rails to be communicated, the one bread and the one cup given by a mixed team of clergy and lay ministers, with a multi-racial choir, servers and sidesmen – all this in apartheid-mad South Africa – then tears sometimes streamed down my cheeks, tears of joy that it could be that indeed Jesus Christ had broken down the wall of partition and here were the first fruits of the eschatological community right in front of my eyes, enacting the message in several languages on the noticeboard outside that this is a house of prayer for peoples of all races who are welcome at all times.

That has been the tremendous witness of St Mary's over the past fifty years. May God bless us in the next fifty to be true to our great tradition and witness powerfully to His redeeming, reconciling, forgiving, welcoming love. Thanks be to God for all His faithful servants who have worshipped Him in St Mary's in those fifty years.

St Mary's has made me believe the vision of St John the Divine:

After this I looked and saw a vast throng, which no one could count, from every nation, of all tribes, peoples and languages, standing in front of the throne and before the Lamb. They were robed in white and had palms in their hands, and they shouted together:

"Victory to our God who sits on the throne, and to the Lamb!" And all the angels stood round the throne and the elders and the four living creatures, and they fell on their faces before the throne and worshipped God, crying: "Amen! Praise and glory and wisdom, thanksgiving and honour, power and might, be to our God for ever and ever, Amen!" (Revelation 7:9–12)

What Jesus Means to Me

One day at a party in England for some reason we were expected to pay for our tea. I offered to buy a cup for an acquaintance. Now he could have said, "No, thank you." You could have knocked me down with a feather when he replied, "No, I won't be subsidized!" Well, I never! I suppose it was an understandable attitude. You want to pay your own way and not sponge on others. But it is an attitude that many have seemed to carry over into our relationship with God – our refusal to be subsidized even by Him. It all stems very much from the prevailing achievement ethic which permeates our very existence. It is drummed into our heads, from our most impressionable days, that you must succeed. At school you must not just do well, no, you must grind the opposition into the dust. We get so worked up that our children can become nervous wrecks as they are egged on to greater efforts by competitive parents. Our culture has it that ulcers have become status symbols. It has got to the stage where the worst sin in our society is to have failed. We don't mind how a person succeeds, or even at what he excels, so long as he succeeds. Then they become superstars. Success is something we *achieve*, it crowns *our* effort and says we have arrived. It serves to massage our ego and says we amount to something, the world testifies to that. Of course this rampant competitiveness takes its toll. We are hagridden by anxiety lest we fail. We worry that we may be inadequate (and often we are – we are like the chap who went to the psychiatrist and said, "Doctor, I think I have an inferiority complex" and the doctor said, "No, you don't have an inferiority complex. You are inferior"). All of us have some inadequacy or other. We prove our maturity by how we deal with that fact. Most of us pretend we aren't inferior and throw our weight around to prove that we count. We work ourselves into a frazzle in order to succeed, in order to be accepted, and we can't understand that we should certainly not carry this attitude over to our relationship with God.

What a tremendous relief it should be, and has been to many, to discover that we don't need to prove ourselves to God. We don't have to do anything at all, to be acceptable to Him. That is what Jesus came to say, and for that He got killed. He came to say, "Hey, you don't have to earn God's love. It is not a matter for human achievement. You exist because God loves you already. You are a child of divine love." The Pharisees, the religious leaders of His day – the bishops and presidents and moderators – they couldn't buy that. Jesus tried to tell them all sorts of stories to prove this point, like the one about the labourers in the vineyard, who were hired in batches at different times of the day. With all but the very last lot the owner of the vineyard came to an agreement about the wages. The last lot worked for no time at all and yet they were paid a full day's wage – God's love and compassion are given freely and without measure, they are not earned. They are totally unmerited and gracious. The religious leaders thought Jesus was proclaiming a thoroughly disreputable God with very low standards – any Tom, Dick and Harry, Mary and Jane would soon be jostling with the prim and proper ones. Stupendously that was true; no, just part of the truth. Jesus was saying that the unlikely ones, those despised ones, the sinners, the prostitutes, the tax collectors, would in fact precede the prim and proper ones into the Kingdom of God. That really set the cat among some ecclesiastical pigeons, I can tell you.

He really scandalized them. He ate with the riffraff and the scum – those were the ones with whom He hobnobbed, because He had come to seek and to find the lost, and as a physician He was needed by those who were sick, not the whole (or those who thought they were whole and righteous). He told the story of the Pharisee and the publican who went to pray. The one boasted to God that he was thankful he was not like other men, especially that publican over there; whereas the publican hardly dared lift his eyes to heaven.

He knew his need, his utter unworthiness, and so he was acceptable to God and received God's gift because he was empty of self.

The Good News is that God loves me long before I could have done anything to deserve it. He is like the father of the prodigal son, waiting anxiously for the return of his wayward son, and when he sees this feckless creature appearing on the horizon, he rushes out to meet him, embrace and kiss him, not recriminating, but asking that the fatted calf be slaughtered, a ring be placed on his finger, and the best robe be put on him; and they must rejoice in a party to celebrate because this lost one has been found, this dead one has come to life again. God is like the good shepherd who goes out looking for the lost sheep. We are misled by the religious pictures which depict Jesus as the good shepherd carrying a cuddly white lamb on His shoulder. A lamb will hardly stray from its mother. It is the troublesome, obstreperous sheep which is likely to go astray, going through the fence, having its wool torn and probably ending up in a ditch of dirty water. It is this dirty, smelling, riotous creature which the Good Shepherd goes after, leaving the good, well-behaved ninety-nine sheep in the wilderness, and when He finds it, why, He carries it on His shoulder and calls His friends to celebrate with Him.

That is tremendous stuff – that is the Good News. Whilst we were yet sinners, says St Paul, Christ died for us. God did not wait until we were die-able, for He could have waited until the cows came home. No, whilst we were God's enemies He accepted us. God loves us, says Jesus, not because we are lovable, but we are lovable because God loves us. That has liberated me to give me the assurance of the child in his father's home. I am loved. That is the most important fact about me and nothing, absolutely nothing, can change that fact. All I do now is an expression of my gratitude for what God has already done for me in Christ Jesus, my Lord and Saviour. Of course, only those who have never loved will say there will be a lowering of standards. When a chap is in love, he will go out in all kinds of weather to keep an appointment with his beloved. Love can be demanding, in fact more demanding than law. It has its own imperatives – think of a mother sitting by the bedside of a sick child through the night, impelled only by love. Nothing is too much trouble for love.

Jesus attests my infinite value as a child of God

In Jeremiah 1:4 we find a strange statement. You could almost say God didn't know much about human biology. But what was He saying to Jeremiah? He wanted to assure him that His call to be a prophet was no divine afterthought, that it was part of God's plan from all eternity. It says that each one of us is part of the divine plan and as such totally irreplaceable and unique. We might some of us look like accidents but we are not accidents for God. No one, not even my identical twin, can love God in exactly the way that I can love God. We are each unique originals not carbon copies. On my birthday my wife gave me a card showing a Darby and Joan couple. On the outside it said, "We have a beautiful and unique relationship", and inside it said, "I am beautiful and you are certainly unique." But have you seen a symphony orchestra? They are all dolled up and beautiful, with their magnificent instruments, cellos, violins, etc. Sometimes, dolled up as the rest, there is a chap at the back carrying a triangle. Now and again the conductor will point to him and he will play "ting". That might seem so insignificant, but in the conception of the composer something irreplaceable would be lost to the total beauty of the symphony if that "ting" did not happen. In the praise ascending to God's throne something totally irreplaceable of your unique way of loving God would be missing. We are each, says Jesus, of unique and inestimable value, so that while He is rushing to the house of Jairus to be with his dying daughter, Jesus must needs stop to attend to the woman with a haemorrhage, or He will speak directly in a crowd to one person, as He did to Zacchaeus. You know something – we are each a temple, a tabernacle, a sanctuary of the Holy Spirit, of Jesus, of God. Yes, you are a God-carrier. God dwells in you He dwells in me, that is why it is such a blasphemy for God's children to be treated as if they were things, uprooted from their homes and dumped in arid resettlement camps. Jesus says that to do something to those He called the least of His brethren is to do it unto Him. My value is intrinsic – i.e., it is constitutive of me as a human being created in the image of God. I am God's viceroy on earth, you are God's viceroy. *Magtig*, if only we could believe this of ourselves then we would behave so differently to our usual conduct. Those who are victims of injustice and oppression would not have to suffer from a slave mentality by which they despised themselves and went about apologizing for their existence. They would know that they matter to God, and nothing anybody did to them could change that fundamental fact about themselves. And those who are privileged would realize that they matter too. They have an intrinsic and inalienable value and so don't need to amass material possessions so obsessionally as if to say 'That is what I am worth – that is who I am'; nor would they have to behave like a bully – his behaviour is really a cry for help, for recognition. They would then have to stop throwing their weight around. God, please help us to know that we matter, that we are creatures of your love, from all eternity, for you chose us in Christ even before the foundation of the world. What bliss, what ecstasy! If we really could believe that, the world would be revolutionized.

Jesus is the affirming one

Often we think of religion as life-denying – as a series of "Don't this and don't the other", as a spoilsport wet-blanket, stopping us from doing the things we most enjoy doing or letting us do them, but with a guilty conscience. There are religious pictures which were popular, certainly in the townships, which showed two sets of people. One set was carrying palm branches and the people were dressed in white, walking in solemn procession towards a great light

141

with hardly a smile on anyone's face. The other group showed people who were having fun, dancing, playing guitars, and cards, and they were all being pitchforked into a red-hot fire by the Devil (who was black) and his angels, who were obviously enjoying themselves.

Let me tell you straight away that that is a travesty of what religion is all about – certainly the religion of Jesus. Jesus was splendidly life-affirming. How else can you explain His concern to heal the sick, to feed the hungry, etc., when He could have said, "Let's pray about it, and it will all be okay upstairs when you die"? He forgave sins, to relieve God's children of all that was unnecessarily burdensome. And He celebrated life and the good things that His Father had created. He rejoiced in the lilies of the field and the birds of the air. He knew that it was all created good, very good according to Genesis. He was often depicted attending dinner parties and weddings, and had provided wine once at a wedding when supplies had run out. He was accused in fact of being a wine-bibber and a friend of sinners. He declared by this open and welcoming attitude to life, that all life, secular and sacred, material and spiritual, belonged to God, came from God and would return to God. Many religious people think that long sulky faces somehow are related to holiness – they often look as though they have taken an unexpected dose of castor oil and find it hard to laugh in church, being somewhat sheepish when they do. And yet Jesus was funny when He described the chap who is concerned to remove a speck of dust from his brother's eye while a huge beam was sticking out of his own. Jesus was poking fun at this chap and His audience would roar with laughter. You often hear people say that the sin Adam and Eve committed must have been related to sex. What utter nonsense! If God said they should be fruitful and multiply, do those people think He expected them to do so by looking into each other's eyes? He, Jesus, celebrated life and He declares all wholesome things good – we are meant to enjoy good food, glorious music, beautiful girls and lovely men, attractive scenery, noble literature, refreshing recreation – they are part of what life is about. Jesus leads us into all truth through His spirit, and therefore as a Christian I glory in the tremendous discoveries of science. I do not see science as a rival or enemy of religion. All truth is of God and can never be self-contradictory. We don't have a God who rules only over the areas of human ignorance, so that as the frontiers of knowledge extend His domain keeps diminishing. No, ours is not a God of the gaps. We say, as we marvel at the discoveries and inventions of science, if man is so wonderful, how much more wonderful must God the creator be. Christians must glory in the strides of human knowledge. Our God does not reign over puny, guilt-ridden, obsequious creatures. He reigns over human beings at their best and most noble, and seeks to help us attain a mature humanity measured by nothing less than the perfect humanity of Christ Himself, the man for others, always a spendthrift for others, ready to suffer the vulnerability of love, willing to be taken advantage of, ready to serve and not be served, to tie a towel round His waist and to wash the disciples' feet. There can be no greater love – because it is only in giving that we receive, it is only in dying that we shall rise to eternal life.

This Jesus affirms me and says I matter, so I can have a proper self-assurance. You know how we all blossom in the presence of one who sees the good in us and who can coax the best out of us. And we know just how we wilt in the company of the person who is for ever finding fault with us. We are sure to break that special cup of the lady who is always fussy about her precious heirlooms. We become all thumbs in her presence. Just note how Jesus was able to get a prostitute like Mary Magdalene to become one of the greatest saints. He mentioned the quality in her which nobody else had noticed – her great capacity to love; and from selling her body she became one of His most loyal followers. Or His treatment of Peter after the resurrection – Peter who had indicated that he would follow Jesus even to death, and then at the precise moment when Jesus needed him most had denied Him three times. Can you imagine what a roasting I would have given to a friend who had left me so badly in the lurch? I would have fairly excoriated him. But Jesus, what does He do? He asks Peter three times whether he loves Him, so that Peter can assert three times that he does, cancelling out the threefold denials. And then Jesus gives this fickle, unpredictable Peter a demanding task – He calls him at another point "rock", this most unrocklike creature.

At the Lambeth Conference we had the privilege of listening to some outstanding devotional addresses, some of the best being by Anthony Bloom, the Orthodox master of the spiritual life. He told us at one point the story of a simple Russian country priest who was confronted by an eminent scientist. This chap trotted out apparently devastating arguments against the existence of God and declared, "I don't believe in God." The unlettered priest retorted quickly, "Oh, it doesn't matter – God believes in you." That is what Jesus says to me – God believes in you. St Paul never ceased to marvel at the Good News of God's unmerited love for us. He described some of what God had done for us – that in baptism we had died and been buried with Christ, that we had risen to a new life of righteousness with Him. Not only that, but that we had already ascended with Christ and staggeringly, unbelievably, we were already reigning with Jesus at the right hand of the Father. Can you believe that – you and I are, despite all appearances to the contrary, princes and princesses together with Christ.

You know, students sometimes don't know the answers to exam questions (not you here!) and they produce those gems called howlers. Once in a scripture exam the students were asked, "What did John the Baptist say to Jesus when He came to be baptized?" Well this chap (I don't think it was a chappess) did not know the answer but was going to have a shot at it, and wrote, "John the Baptist said to Jesus 'Remember you are the Son of God and behave like one!'"

Well, remember you are princes and princesses, God's loved ones – behave like one.

University of Natal, Durban
6 and 7 August 1981

Feast for Epiphany

At the sight of the star they were overjoyed. (Matthew 2:10)

We are still observing the Feast of the Epiphany – the showing forth of Jesus to the nations or the Gentiles who were represented by the wise men from the East.

I remember that in the past if you were what is called high church, then you used to genuflect at the words from the Epiphany Gospel – and often "they fell down and worshipped Him". You and I know that human beings such as ourselves have very many characteristics. For instance, we are usually inquisitive. If we hear loud voices of people like Mr & Mrs Jones quarrelling next door, then we are quick to go to our windows to spy out what is happening. And of course, when on the following day we see Mrs Jones sporting a black eye, we know how she got it, but we may ask her what happened and she may tell us that she fell over the cat and struck her head against the table – but then, we know better.

Now another characteristic that we all have is the need to worship – to worship something or someone greater than ourselves, to whom we wish to dedicate our whole lives unreservedly. Sometimes they say we all have a God-shaped space inside us and only God can fill it. This means that we are created by God, we are created like God, and we are created for God. And since God is infinite, you and I are made for the infinite and nothing less than God can ever really satisfy our hunger for God. St Augustine of Hippo, the great and learned African saint, once said, "Thou hast made us for Thyself and our hearts are restless until they find their rest in Thee."

Others try to worship things that are less than God – it may be money, or ambition, or drugs or sex. In the end they find that these are worthless idols. To worship means to give due worth to someone or something. We give worth to God. Worship is absolutely central to our faith where God comes first always. We bow before His infinite majesty and holiness, trembling with awe at His unapproachable light and radiance, before which the angels and the archangels veil their sight, whom we join, as in this service, in their heavenly praise and adoration, as they cry ceaselessly, "Holy, Holy, Holy, Lord God of Hosts, Heaven and earth are full of Thy glory." Many times we feel words are utterly inadequate, so we keep a deep silence in this holy presence. If we do not have this capacity to wonder and adore then we must perish. We are moved to worship by the splendour of the rising or the setting sun, by the grandeur of snowcapped mountains, by the awesome wonder of the billowing sea, by a flower with dew drops on its petals opening to the sun, by the unspeakable wonder of a baby being born. Yes, all this and more moves us to cry, "How great and wonderful Thou art, Lord God Almighty." And yet such worship can be hollow and a form of escapism from the harsh realities of life as we and many others live it, with its poverty, hunger and anxiety about rent and other matters. But true Christian worship can never let us be indifferent to the needs of others, to the cries of the hungry, of the naked and the homeless, of the sick and the prisoner, of the oppressed and the disadvantaged. Our Lord said, "As much as you have done this [i.e. fed the hungry, clothed the naked, visited the sick and the prisoners] to the least of my brethren, you have done it to me, and in as much as you have not done it to the least of these my brethren you have not done it to me."

True Christian worship includes the love of God and the love of neighbour. The two must go together or your Christianity is false. St John asks, in his First Epistle, how you can say you love God whom you have not seen if you hate your brother whom you have. Our love for God is tested and proved by our love for our neighbour. This is what the churches, and perhaps especially the South African Council of Churches, attempt to do in that beautiful but sadly unhappy land which is South Africa. It has a vicious political system of segregation called apartheid. There are many victims of this system: the family who are bereft of their father who must be a migrant labourer in the White man's cities, living in single-sex hostels, the persons who provide cheap unskilled labour to swell investment income; the marginalized, the disadvantaged who are treated often as objects and not subjects. Many have protested against this system and for their pains they are often detained for long periods without trial, or banned for five years at a time to a twilight existence when they can't attend any gathering. A gathering, I would have you know, is more than one person, so they can't speak to more than one person at a time, and they can't be quoted; others are brought to trial under a system where you are presumed guilty until you can prove you are innocent. These detained persons, these banned people, these political prisoners, are the least of Christ's brothers and sisters He referred to, and we try, with the very generous help of people overseas, to minister to them – this we contend is deeply religious work, others call it political.

I visited one of these banned people, Winnie Mandela. Her husband, Nelson Mandela, is serving a life sentence on Robben Island, our maximum security prison. I wanted to take her Holy Communion. The police told me I couldn't enter her house. So we celebrated Holy Communion in my car in the street, in Christian South Africa. On a second occasion I went to see her on a weekend. Her restriction order is more strict at weekends. She can't leave her yard. So we celebrated Holy Communion again in the street. This time Winnie was on one side of the fence and I on the other. This in Christian South Africa in 1978.

We are Christian not only in church on Sunday. Our Christianity is not something we put on, like our Sunday best, only for Sundays. It is for every day. We are Christians from Monday to Monday. We have no off day. We are Christians at play, at work and at prayer. They are all rolled into one. It is not *either* worship *or* trying to do all the good works in our community. It is both. The wise men came to the Child and worshipped. Then they gave Him their gifts. We too must worship our God for ever and ever, and serve Him by serving our neighbour today and always. What would you do today to fulfil this Christian duty?

World Council of Churches Central Committee
Kingston, Jamaica
1979

Love Reveals My Neighbour

Men almost always give the impression that they are the bosses, especially at home, but all the while they know who the real bosses are. Many are described as male chauvinist pigs really only because they are trying to bolster their sagging morale by throwing their weight about, or at least trying to do so. I remember a story of the man who was driving behind a car that was moving somewhat erratically. So he exclaimed, "It must be one of those stupid women drivers!" His wife sat unconcerned next to him. They overtook the offending car and, lo and behold, the driver was a man! Quite undaunted, the driver who had made the disparaging remark about women drivers said, "I'm sure he was taught by his mother!"

Often too, in reference to the story of Adam and Eve, men will say, "We are in the mess we find ourselves in because of a woman, Eve, who succumbed to the blandishments pointed out by the snake." I suppose women could say, "Uhmm, yes, that is probably true, but what would have been our plight if Mary had refused to become the mother of Our Lord Jesus Christ?"

If it took a woman to get us into trouble, then it took a woman to get us out of trouble. Jesus could not have been born unless a woman had agreed to co-operate with God. I have said that as a preamble to underline that I believe you have a tremendous role to play, that you are playing a tremendous role. It is utterly true that behind every

149

successful man there is a woman. Perhaps it should be not *behind* but *beside* (and, after all, the hand that rocks the cradle, they say, rules the world!).

There is a little piece about Eve and Adam's rib which we would do well to ponder. It speaks about how woman was created not out of man's footbone in order to be trampled underfoot, nor out of his headbone so as to dominate him, but out of his rib so that she could share his chief concerns as an equal side by side with him. Subordination is not the same thing as inferiority. Sometimes the subordinate is superior to the one to whom he is subordinate.

Just a few words about your theme – "Love reveals my neighbour, my responsibility." When you look at someone with eyes of love, you see a reality different from that of someone who looks at the same person without love, with hatred or even just with indifference. You who are mothers know that hardly any one of you here would ever admit openly that your child was ugly or ill-behaved (perhaps you might say it yourselves, but would resent it if anybody else ventured to make that observation). Even if your child were to have been caught red-handed in misbehaviour, and the police had come to your house and found stolen goods, when people asked what had happened most parents would say, "They say he has stolen clothes." English expressions which say much of what I have been at pains to describe are: "Possession turns sand into gold" and "Beauty is in the eye of the beholder." Enough of that.

When we read the story of the Good Samaritan we often think of the priest and the Levite as cruel, uncaring people. But I think we make a big mistake if we do. They were not particularly bad people. They did have genuine reasons. They were rushing to go to the Temple in Jerusalem to attend the services. If they stopped, they would be late for those important services and they would become ritually unclean, which would make them unfit to participate in the worship of the Temple and that would be taking away something due to God. Let us translate it into contemporary terms. Here is a Bishop who must get to the cathedral because it is ordination Sunday. The cathedral he knows is packed, and nothing can go on without him. Then rushing past, he sees someone injured by the roadside. If he stops he does not know how long he is likely to be delayed. Is that man more important than all those people waiting in the cathedral? Or someone working at Leratong or Baragwanath – a nursing sister; can she afford to be late and risk at least a rebuke or worse an expulsion or disciplinary action of some sort or other? Well, the Good Samaritan did not see him as a case, he saw him as a brother, as a neighbour.

It is interesting that Jesus was asked the question, "Who is my neighbour?", and the questioner hoped that Jesus would say, "Your neighbour is so and so and not so and so," i.e. the definition would be an exclusivist one, building boundaries for the exercise of neighbourly concern. Note the answer Jesus gave – He described someone in need and someone who gave help to the one in need and two people who didn't. And then He asked a question in return in true Socratic fashion, so that the person addressed would discover the truth for himself. Now the radical point about Jesus' question is that He asks who proved a *neighbour* to the man in need.

You are gathered here and are in fact not going round to discover who your neighbour is (whom you are supposed to love as yourself, as the second great commandment says). No, you are meant to be asking "To whom am I going to be a neighbour? – Who is in need and whose need must I meet as a neighbour with this privilege and this responsibility?" You and I are the ones who are to be judged for failing to be a neighbour to those in need.

We live in a country that has many casualties and disasters. Some of these are naturally caused, but many are caused by man in his inhumanity to his fellow man. Today a certain section of South Africa is celebrating that God gave them a racial victory over another group of people, and that thereby God gave them superiority over all the peoples of South Africa, to do as they wished with them. They speak about self-determination for everyone, except that they have unilaterally decided how that self-determination must happen. If, for instance, people said they do not want Bantustans or Bantu Education, then those in power reject these desires as Communism. They are like those who say, "You are free to choose any colour you like as long as it is white." So we have a vicious, evil, unchristian policy in South Africa and it is causing suffering to many people. It produces banned people, detained without trial people, uprooted and dumped people in the resettlement areas, starving people, it produces hostel people, delinquent people, and pensioners who can't make ends meet. They are just a few of those in need. I can't prescribe what you must do. You have to have the sensitivity of love not to hurt people's pride. Don't be a do-gooder. Sometimes all that is necessary is to visit a banned or detained person and show that you do not fear contamination and that you don't fear the system. You mothers ultimately will be the ones who must play a significant role to destroy apartheid. As Mrs Sisulu asked at Mr Mxenge's funeral, how many of your children must go into exile, be banned, be detained and be killed before you can do anything about it? Because a lot of the need in South Africa is artificially and deliberately induced. It should not be there. It won't be there when apartheid has disappeared.

May God bless you in your deliberations and at Christmas and in 1982. May you be a true neighbour to all in need whom love will show you.

Address to Women's Group
December 1981

152

The Divine Intention

Preamble
My Lord and members of the Eloff Commission, I want to start by expressing the appreciation of the South African Council of Churches to the Commission and its officers in their dealings with the Council. They could very well have hamstrung our operations by taking away our books and records. Instead they examined our records in such a way as to dislocate our work as little as possible – for this we are grateful.

Secondly, I want to indicate briefly at the beginning what I hope to elaborate in the body of my submission.

My purpose is to demonstrate from the Scriptures and from hallowed Christian tradition and teaching that what we are as the South African Council of Churches, what we say and what we do, all of these are determined not by politics or any other ideology. We are what we are in obedience to God and in response to the gracious Gospel of His Son, Our Lord and Saviour Jesus Christ. Ultimately we owe loyalty not to any human authority, however prestigious or powerful, but to God and to His Son, Our Lord Jesus Christ alone, from whom we obtain our mandate. We must obey the divine imperative and word whatever the cost.

Everything we do or say and everything we are must be tested by whether it is consistent with the Gospel of Jesus Christ or not, and not by whether it is merely expedient or even acceptable to the Government of the day or whether it is popular. To understand the nature of the Council, its aims, objectives and activities requires that you appreciate the theological *raison d'être* of its existence. Without this biblical and theological justification you will almost certainly misunderstand what we are about. Consequently, I want to underline that it is not the finances or any other activities of the SACC that are being investigated. It is our Christian faith, it is the Christian churches who are members of the SACC who are on trial. It is our Christianity, it is our faith and therefore our theology that are under scrutiny, and the central matters at issue are profoundly theological. As a Commission you are being asked to determine whether our understanding and practice of the Christian faith can pass muster. We are on trial for being Christian, and that by a Government which itself claims to be Christian. It may be that we are being told that it is an offence to be a Christian in South Africa. That is what you are asked to determine. And that is a theological task through and through.

I will show that the Bible describes God as creating the universe to be a cosmos and not a chaos, a cosmos in which harmony, unity, order, fellowship, communion, peace and justice would reign and that this divine intention was disturbed by sin. The result was disunity, alienation, disorder, chaos, separation, and in the face of this God then sent His Son to restore that primordial harmony to effect reconciliation.

By becoming a real human being through Jesus Christ, God showed that He took the whole of human history and the whole of human life seriously. He demonstrated that He was Lord of all Life, spiritual and secular, sacred and profane, material and spiritual. We will show that Scripture and the main stream of Christian tradition and teaching know nothing of the dichotomies so popular in our day, which demand the separation of religion from politics, etc These I will demonstrate are deeply theological matters which affect the nature, work and attitudes of the SACC. Our God cares that children starve in resettlement camps, the somewhat respectable name for apartheid's dumping grounds for the pathetic casualties of this vicious and evil system. The God we worship does care that people die mysteriously in detention. He is concerned that people are condemned to a twilight existence as non-persons by an arbitrary bureaucratic act of banning, without giving them the opportunity to reply to charges brought against them. I will show this from the Bible. I might add that if God did not care about these and similar matters, I would not worship Him, for He would be a totally useless God. Mercifully, He is not such a God.

I will soon show that the central work of Jesus was to effect reconciliation between God and us and also between man and man. Consequently, from a theological and scriptural base, I will demonstrate that apartheid, separate development or whatever it is called, is evil, totally and without remainder, that it is unchristian and unbiblical. It has recently been declared a heresy by a world body of responsible Christians, a body to which the White Dutch Reformed Churches belong and which can therefore not be dismissed as a so-called left-wing radical body, unless you want to use these epithets of the NGK as well, since they have been hurt that their membership of this august body, whose President is present in this Court this morning, has been suspended. If anyone were to show me that apartheid is biblical or Christian, I have said before, and I reiterate now, that I would burn my Bible and cease to be Christian. I will want to show that the Christian Bible and the Gospel of Jesus Christ Our Lord is subversive of all injustice and evil, oppression and exploitation, and that God is on the side of the oppressed and the downtrodden, that He is the liberator God of the Exodus, who leads His people out of every kind of bondage, spiritual, political, social and economic, and nothing will thwart Him from achieving the goal of the liberation of all His people and the whole of His creation.

The SACC and its member churches, we will show, are not a tuppenny ha'penny fly-by-night organization. We belong to the Church of God, a Church that is found universally, spread out throughout the face of the whole inhabited universe. That is what the Greek word from which we find "ecumenical" means. It is the Body of Jesus Christ of which we are members, and it is a supernatural, a divine fellowship brought into being by the action of God Himself through His Holy Spirit. It is not merely a human organization that is limited by national or ethnic boundaries. It transcends time and space, race, culture and sex, nationality and all the things that men sometimes think are important. I am a bishop in the Church of God – that is what was pronounced over me when I was consecrated – so that I am a bishop of the Church when I go to Timbuktoo, when I go to Korea; I am a bishop of the Church in Russia and in the United States. We belong to something which includes the living in what is called "the Church militant", which includes the dead in what is called "the Church quiescent", which includes the saints in glory in what is called "the Church triumphant". Theologically I have brothers and sisters whom I have never met physically and will probably never meet, but ontologically we are one in Our Lord Jesus Christ, and I know that they are upholding us with their prayers, with their love, with their caring concern even now. Your investigators will know that from their recent visit in the United States. Because of this theological fact of the nature of the Church we express our oneness in all kinds of ways – in our prayers for one another, in making up what is lacking in the resources of another church, and so on. When one church gives to another church either personnel, or material, or money resources that is in fact nothing remarkable. It is as it should be. It is an expression of Christian fellowship, of *koinonia* in Our Lord.

156

We might want local churches to be more self-supporting but it is no aberration for a more affluent part of the Church to give of its wealth, of which it is only a steward on behalf of God from whom all things come. It gives and it receives. There is the mutuality of giving and receiving, as of a loving family. Those who criticize the SACC for depending so greatly on overseas support show their woeful ignorance of ecclesiology, the theology of the nature of the Church of God – when one part suffers the whole suffers with it and when one part rejoices the whole rejoices with it.

Thirdly, I have already said we owe our ultimate loyalty and allegiance only to God. With due respect I want to submit that no secular authority nor its appointed Commissions has any competence whatsoever to determine how a church is a church nor what is the nature of the Gospel of Jesus Christ. When a secular authority tries to do this then it is usurping divine prerogatives and the prerogatives of the Church itself. With respect, we do not recognize the right of the Commission to inquire into our theological existence, and, therefore, into any aspect of our life as a Council, since every aspect of our existence is determined by theological facts, as I have already pointed out. Only our member churches can call us to task. If we have contravened any laws of the country then you don't need a Commission to determine that. There is an array of draconian laws at the disposal of the Government, and the Courts of Law are the proper place to determine our guilt or innocence. This Commission, with respect, is totally superfluous. We have agreed to appear before it only because we have nothing to hide, which does not mean that we are infallible. Our written submission to the Commission acknowledges that we are fallible and have made mistakes, but it is our member churches and not the Government or any other secular authority who are the proper judges of that. And to reveal that we are sinners, as if some major scientific discovery was being made, is to become quite ridiculous in Christian terms for it is to labour the obvious. We are always justified and we are always sinners. We depend not on our goodness but on the gracious mercy of God. And again the Government or any other secular body has no competence whatsoever to pass judgement on this. God alone can do that. And when the Government usurps God's prerogative then it becomes not just wrong, but blasphemous.

The Government appointed this Commission for a reason that is perfectly obvious and totally unsubtle. It has used Commissions before to deal with awkward customers. I don't impugn the integrity of this Commission and its members in any way, but I want the Government to know now and always that I do not fear them. They are trying to defend the utterly indefensible. Apartheid is as evil and as vicious as Nazism and Communism, and the Government will fail completely for it is ranging itself on the side of evil, injustice and oppression. The Government is not God, they are just ordinary human beings who very soon – like other tyrants before them – will bite the dust. When they take on the SACC they must know that they are taking on the Church of God, and those who have done so in the past, the Neros, the Hitlers, the Amins of this world, have ended up, as I have said before on another occasion, as the flotsam and jetsam of history. Christ has assured us that His Church is founded on rock and not even the gates of Hell can prevail against it. The Resurrection of Our Lord and Saviour declares for all to know that life will triumph over darkness, that goodness will triumph over evil, that justice will triumph over injustice, and that freedom will triumph over tyranny. I stand before you as one who believes fervently what Paul wrote when he said, "If God be for us, who can be against us?"

The divine intention
In the Constitution of the SACC under the heading
OBJECTS we read:

> The principal objects of the Council shall be:
> 3.1 To foster that unity which is both God's will for all
> mankind and His gift to the Church.

I want to point out that this first object permeates all the
other objects, reflected in expressions such as "to co-ordinate
the work in Southern Africa of churches", "to undertake on
behalf of churches . . . joint action and service . . . and to
encourage joint action and service . . ."; "to do all such things
to encourage all such things . . . calculated to reduce divisive
factors . . ."; "by developing dialogue with people of other
faiths and ideologies".

It can be said that the search for the unity of the Church
and of humankind is a central concern of the SACC. But is
unity a central biblical concern or is it just peripheral to the
life of faith, something to be engaged in as an optional extra
by those who are temperamentally suited to do so? I want to
show that the SACC and its member churches have their
agenda and their programmes in this matter determined by
what the Scriptures have revealed as the will of God, the God
and Father of Our Lord Jesus Christ. I want to stress that this
concern for unity is not something that was introduced by the
ecumenical movement from its inception. No, the Scriptures
declare that unity; the unity of the entire creation was God's
intention from the very beginning of creation. The SACC is
thus caught up in a divine mission; it is a fellow worker with
none other than God Himself; it is an agent of the divine
mercy and compassion and concern not just for the world and
not just for human beings, but for the whole of creation.

Let us start at the beginning where the Bible seems to

159

start, and that is with the creation of all there is. We find our sources in the sublime stories contained in the first eleven chapters of Genesis. Some have sought to dismiss these stories as myths, meaning that their truth content was no more than that of fairy tales. But those who do so are dull, unimaginative souls who would ask Wordsworth – writing about a host of golden daffodils "dancing in the breeze" – which band was playing, and who were their dancing partners. No, in these chapters we have the evocative, imaginative, highly symbolical language of poetry conveying to us some of the most profound theological, or if you like, spiritual and existential truths about God, about ourselves and about the rest of God's creation, and no advances in technology or science will be able to produce anything to contradict those truths – true science cannot contradict true religion.

The first creation narrative reaches a climax in Genesis 1:26 when God says, "Let us create man in our image and likeness to rule . . ." Human beings are created, so St Augustine of Hippo tells us, by God, like God, for God. God creates man to become His viceroy, His representative to rule over the rest of creation on God's behalf. In olden times the Emperor's statue received the same honour and respect as the Emperor himself and represented him where he could not travel in his vast domains. That is the high privilege bestowed on each human person, male and female, as the passage goes on to explain – that each human being is God's own representative, own viceroy or ambassador, and no mention is made of race or nationality or colour. It is the fact of their being created by God that endows them with this infinite and eternal value. But note also that they are expected to rule over the rest of creation on behalf of God. So already in those early verses of the Bible we get definite adumbrations of the Kingdom of God, about which the New Testament is so explicit and to which I want to refer later.

160

May I point out that the biblical author depicts the primal state of affairs as being such that harmony, unity, fellowship and friendliness abound. Poetically and symbolically this is done by saying that every living creature was at this stage a vegetarian. There was no bloodshed in God's creation according to His will and intention. There was no bloodshed, not even for blood sacrifices. Nature was not yet red in tooth and claw.

The second creation story speaks about the idyllic paradise of Eden in which Adam and Eve lived happily. There was abundant food. Adam named the animals to demonstrate his hegemony over all creation. Adam and Eve were as innocents abroad, communicating directly with God, who visited them as a man visits his friends, "walking with them in the garden in the cool of the evening". The animals did not prey on each other. The lion gambolled with the lamb. The picture we have is of a creation at peace, abounding in harmony, unity and fellowship. This was God's intention for the entire universe because unity means peace, prosperity, fellowship, justice, wholeness, compassion, love and joy *et al.* conveyed in the virtually untranslatable Hebrew word *Shalom*. It was a condition in which God's will was being done, in which His laws were being obeyed.

The Bible declares that things then went horribly, badly wrong because sin entered God's creation. There is no speculation about the origin of sin. We have a phenomenological account of what followed in the train of sin. The primal unity was disrupted. Where there was unity, there was now disunity, harmony was replaced by disharmony. There was alienation and hatred and enmity. Fellowship and communion were destroyed, and it was not just humankind that was affected: the rest of creation fell with the human beings. The ground brought forth thistles. There was murder and death (Cain/Abel), war and strife. And the Genesis stories culminate in the shattering story of

161

the Tower of Babel, where human community and fellowship become impossible – human beings can no longer communicate with one another because God has confused their languages and people are torn apart. That is the ultimate consequence, according to the Bible, of sin, separation, alienation, apartness. It is a perverse exegesis that would hold that the story of the Tower of Babel is a justification for racial separation, a divine sanction for the diversity of nations. It is to declare that the divine punishment of sin had become the divine intention for humankind. That is a position the Bible would not support.

The entire situation at the end of the story of the Tower of Babel cried out for reconciliation, for atonement. Please note that this word atonement is also at-one-ment, meaning at-one-ing, the reconciling of those who are separated, divided; reconciliation means creating friendship, bringing together, uniting those who formerly were at variance, who were enemies before, who were alienated.

The story of the Bible could be said to be the story of God's mission to restore the harmony which was there at the beginning, when His rule, His reign would be acknowledged once again. This is the divine movement and activity in which the SACC is involved as it prays and works for the unity of the churches and of humankind.

The Scriptures reveal on occasion this nostalgia for Paradise Lost in a Paradise Regained. In the descriptions of the age to come, called the Messianic age (after Messiah, God's Anointed Representative to inaugurate God's rule, God's Kingdom), we hear echoes of the time of the beginning.

So Isaiah in Chapter 11 says of the Anointed One:

He shall judge the poor with justice and defend the humble in the land with equity; his mouth shall be a rod to strike down the ruthless, and with a word he shall slay the wicked. Round his waist he shall wear the belt of justice, and good faith shall be the girdle round his body.

Note the following verses:

> Then the wolf shall live with the sheep, and the leopard lie down with the kid; the calf and the young lion shall grow up together, and a little child shall lead them; the cow and the bear shall be friends, and their young shall lie down together. The lion shall eat straw like cattle; the infant shall play over the hole of the cobra, and the young child dance over the viper's nest. They shall not hurt or destroy in all my holy mountain; for as the waters fill the sea, so shall the land be filled with the knowledge of the Lord. (Isaiah 11:4–9)

Noting this characteristic of looking back in their looking forward, Herman Gunkel, a German biblical scholar, said, "*Endzeit ist Urzeit*" – the end time is as the time of the beginning!

And so God sent His Son to effect reconciliation, to bring about the atonement that would achieve the unity, harmony, peace, justice, fellowship, friendliness, compassion, wholeness which were His intention for His creation from the very beginning. St Paul says, "God was in Christ reconciling the world to Himself" (2 Corinthians 5:19).

Jesus, speaking about His coming crucifixion, declares: "I, if I be lifted up will draw all men to me" (John 12:32), underlining that His chief work in the salvation of the world would be a uniting, a reconciling one. And we must recall that Christian tradition, referring to Christ's seamless robe, speaks of it as symbolizing the unity of the Church and so of all humankind. And in St John's gospel is to be found what tradition speaks of as the High Priestly prayer of Our Lord, as recorded in the seventeenth chapter, and the heart of that

163

prayer is the petition that His followers will be one, with a unity that reflects the unity that subsists between the Father and the Son (John 17:11, 20–23); the unity is not for merely pragmatic reasons that it is economical to have one church building rather than several serving the same community and locality, but because a divided Church is a scandal, making it difficult for people to believe the Gospel of God's love.

The SACC is concerned for unity in all its aspects because it exists to proclaim the Good News of God's love for His world, for which He gave His only begotten Son, in obedience to the commission Our Lord gave to His followers when He said, "Full authority in heaven and earth has been committed to me. Go forth therefore and make all nations my disciples; baptize men everywhere in the Name of the Father and the Son and the Holy Spirit and teach them to observe all that I commanded you. And be assured I am with you always, to the end of time." It is because, as St Paul declares, "God has reconciled us men to Himself through Christ, and He has enlisted us in this service of reconciliation" etc. (2 Corinthians 5:18–21). We are engaged in the ministry of proclaiming the love of God for all His people through the death and resurrection of Jesus Christ Our Lord, and to proclaim the message of reconciliation which is another aspect of unity, of peace, of harmony, of justice, of compassion, of love, of brotherliness. That is why in its organizational structure the SACC has a Division of Mission and Evangelism, which was established to help the churches in their proclamation of the Christian Gospel through word and deed and the concern to win men and women for Christ, so that converted by the Holy Spirit they would accept Jesus and acknowledge Him as their Lord and Master and their Saviour.

We are concerned for justice, but that is a biblical concern. And we are also concerned about and work for reconciliation. And we have a division called the Division of Justice and

Reconciliation, to work for real peace and brotherhood in our land and throughout the world. I will return to this later.

St Paul waxes quite indignant when he thinks the unity of the Christian community has been jeopardized or undermined. In his First Letter to the Corinthians, he is supposed to be responding to questions that the Corinthian church has asked, but because of the disquieting news of factions and divisions in that church, Paul spends the first six chapters dealing with this matter of divisiveness before he deals with their other problems in the next nine chapters. That is strange conduct unless unity was of paramount importance. And he stresses that the Church is the body of Christ endowed with different spiritual and other gifts (*charismata*), having different limbs and organs with different functions – but all designed to function for the good and the benefit of the whole. He stresses the unity, the harmony, the oneness. It is a body in which the natural distinctions of race, status, sex, culture are of no moment any longer. They have been transcended in Jesus Christ Our Lord. He mentions this fact first in 1 Corinthians 12:12–13, and then again in Galatians 3:26–28.

This was what attracted the first converts when they saw this amazing spectacle of Christian *koinonia* and were led to exclaim, "How these Christians love one another!" St Paul exhorts Christians to have the mind of Christ, in Philippians, in order to maintain this precious thing – this unity.

In Ephesians we learn that this was God's intention. Ephesians 1:10 tells of a return to the primordial time of the beginning; and this is what Paul says in Romans 8:19–22.

That is the divine movement in which the SACC and its member churches are caught up. It is to demonstrate in our lives that the Jesus whom we worship as Lord and Master has, as Ephesians declares, broken down the wall of partition which separated Jew from Gentile (Ephesians 2:11–22). This movement, this divine activity, is for bringing together, for

165

uniting, for reconciling, for atoning. Teilhard de Chardin, the French Jesuit paleontologist, spoke of much the same thing when he said that the whole of creation was moving from a point alpha to its goal in the point omega.

The only separation the Bible knows is between believers on the one hand and unbelievers on the other. Any other kind of separation, division, disunity is of the Devil. It is evil and from sin.

Do I still need to demonstrate that apartheid is evil after all that I have said about the centrality for the Bible of unity and reconciliation?

Apartheid is evil for at least three reasons:

• The Bible declares right at the beginning that human beings are created in the image and likeness of God. I showed why this fact endows each person with a unique and infinite value, a person whose very hairs are numbered. And what makes any human being valuable therefore is not any biological characteristic. No, it is the fact that he or she is created in the image and likeness of God. Apartheid exalts a biological quality, which is a total irrelevancy, to the status of what determines the value, the worth of a human being.

Why should skin colour or race be any more useful as a criterion than, say, the size of one's nose? What has the size of my nose to do with whether I am intelligent, etc.? It has no more to do with my worth as a human being than has the colour of my eyes.

• Secondly, the chief work that Jesus came to perform on earth can be summed up in the word "Reconciliation". I have already demonstrated that in what has gone before. He came to restore human community and brotherhood which sin destroyed. He came to say that God had intended us for fellowship, for *koinonia*, for togetherness, without destroying our distinctiveness, our cultural otherness. Apartheid quite deliberately denies and repudiates this central act of Jesus and says we are made for separateness, for disunity, for enmity, for alienation, which we have shown to be the fruits of sin. For this reason alone apartheid is totally unchristian and unbiblical, for it denies not just a peripheral matter but a central verity of the Christian faith.

Professor J. Durand in his response to Professor J. Heyns' article in *Stormkompas* has these words to say:

> The fact that the irreconcilability of people does not pass by the churches is more than just an unfortunate state of affairs. Basically we are concerned here with a contradiction of the nature of the Church. If I read Ephesians 2 correctly, in which the Apostle Paul deals with the partition of separation, which is eliminated in Christ, then the mere existence of the Church is already a negation of the artificial and ideological separation of the people. How is it still possible that such separation can be preached and lived as the will of God and in accordance with the Gospel?

It is to the credit of the *Nederduitse Gereformeerde Sendingkerk in Suid-Afrika* that it channelled the problem of the South African society back to its theological core – reconciliation – at the session of the synod in Belhar in 1978. The decision reads, "The Church wishes to express as its conviction that the apartheid policy and/or separate development such as that upheld by the authorities is contrary to the Gospel:

1. Because as opposed to the Gospel of Christ's objective, which is the reconciliation of man with God and with his fellow man, the forced separation of people on the basis of race and colour is most deeply founded upon the conviction of the fundamental irreconcilability between people who are separate in such a way;

2. Because the system that is evident from such a policy

necessarily had to lead and led to an increasing polarization between people, especially because practice showed that within the system one sector of the population, viz. the Whites, is privileged and that consequently the requirement of the Gospel that justice apply to all has not been met, and

3. Because not only the dignity of the unprivileged sectors of the population is affected but also the dignity of everyone concerned with it."

One sometimes has the impression that those people in, e.g., the Dutch Reformed Church who do know about the above decision dismiss it too lightly as just another example of a decision by a church against apartheid. But the theological implications of this decision cannot be ignored. As a result of it a deeply penetrating question is directed to the church or churches who maintain that the policy mentioned can in some way or another be supported or backed theologically. These churches (and all churches together with it) are asked about the truth of their own church-being in South Africa.

• Thirdly, when moralists are uncertain about the moral quality of an act, etc., then they will ask what the consequences of that particular act or policy or whatever are. If the consequences are evil, then the act being evaluated is declared to be evil. Apartheid treats human beings, God's children, as if they were less than this. It manipulates persons and treats them as if they were means to some end. Immanuel Kant declared that a human person is always an end, never a means to an end.

I said that in the Old Testament we already had foreshadowings of the teaching about the Kingdom of God, for instance in man acting on behalf of God to rule over all creation. It was God's intention to rule as sovereign Lord, and in His Kingdom He was absolute ruler and He demanded undivided loyalty to Himself alone. That is why Israel, His chosen people, are constantly castigated by God's spokesmen, the prophets, for their disloyalty which is likened to adultery since Israel is married to Yahweh, God alone. The Devil and the powers of evil have usurped God's rule and, as it were, God has permitted them to set up their counter kingdom. This world is in the power and control of the evil one, consequently there is evil, war, disease and death. God's children – many of them are held in bondage and in shackles by the evil one and his minions. But God would intervene through His Messiah, the long-expected One, the Anointed One, and when He came He would inaugurate the Kingdom of God. It is this long-awaited One who is referred to in the earlier quotation from Isaiah, who will be imbued with God's spirit. Christians believe that this Promised Messiah has come in Jesus Christ Our Lord.

We believe that God has intervened decisively in and through Jesus Christ, who is very God Himself and yet who became a real human being in that act of stupendous divine condescension called the Incarnation – God becoming man. By this act, God declared that human history is important, and that all of human life is important.

God declared that He is a jealous God brooking no rival whatsoever: "I am the Lord your God and you shall have no other gods beside Me." But He was and is the Lord of all life. When Jesus came and found people who were sick or hungry or naked – He did not send them away with a pious "We will pray about it". No, He fed the hungry, He healed the sick, He cleansed the lepers, He drove out demons. And in doing all of these things, He was demonstrating the presence of His Father's Kingdom (Luke 11:14–20). When the imprisoned John the Baptist asked whether Jesus was indeed the Messiah, Jesus pointed to the things that He was doing, including physical, material things, here and now, as signs of the Kingdom (Luke 7:18–23). All of these things were thoroughly religious and spiritual but many of them were so physical, so material, so secular, so profane. Jesus applied to Himself words out of the book of the prophet Isaiah in His first recorded sermon, as words that aptly summed up His mission (Luke 4).

I want to underline that these are thoroughly political, thoroughly mundane things. If we are to say that religion cannot be concerned with politics then we are really saying that there is a substantial part of human life in which God's writ does not run. If it is not God's then whose is it? Who is in charge if not the God and Father of Our Lord Jesus Christ?

On the Church and politics we could say much, much more. Is it not interesting just how often people and churches are accused of mixing religion with politics? – almost always whenever they condemn a particular social political dispensation as being unjust. If the South African Council of Churches were to say now that it thought apartheid was not so bad, I am as certain as anything that we would not be finding ourselves where we are today. Why is it not being political for a religious body or a religious leader to praise a social political dispensation?

I need to point out that in the Old Testament God was first experienced by the Israelites in the event of the Exodus. That was how they came into contact with God. They were at the time just a rabble of slaves. They did not encounter God in some religious event such as a sacrifice or at worship; He revealed Himself in helping them to escape from bondage, and what could be more political than helping captives to escape? And it is this political event of the Exodus which becomes the founding event of the people of God. It becomes the paradigmatic event of the Bible, so that, looking at what God did in the Exodus, they extrapolate backwards and say

that a God who did so and so, must clearly be the God, the
Lord of creation; and they can extrapolate forwards and say
that a God who can choose a people in this way, must be a
God who has a purpose for them, and that is why we said at
the beginning that God has taken human history seriously,
unlike the nature gods. And when God redeemed us in Our
Lord and Saviour Jesus Christ, it was not through a religious
event. No, it was through an act of execution, used against
common criminals, a judicial event that would be
sanctioned, not by the ecclesiastical leaders, but by the
political ruler in Judea.

I want to quote some strange words. I will explain
afterwards where they come from, M'Lord. I start on
paragraph 2 and the heading is *Rest in the Status Quo*:

The other extreme however is still more fatal to the
Church's effective witness to the world, and that is
acquiescence in unjust conditions. Silence may never be
kept about the social implications of the Gospel of Christ.
There can be little doubt that the present low level of the
spiritual life is in no small measure due to the dilution of
the eternal principles. The whole Church longs and prays
for a revival, but is it psychologically sound to expect
enthusiastic, joyful spiritual life among those living in
misery, hunger and privation? Moses and Aaron also
claimed to quicken new hope and courage in the hearts of
their enslaved people, but what do we read in Exodus 6:8?
But they did not listen to Moses on account of the
despondency and cruel bondage.

The Charge against the Church: The strongest charge
against the Church is born exactly out of the conception
of many that she has not grieved over the ruin of Joseph,
but acquiesced in this in the conditions of injustice,
exploitation and coercion. The Evangelical Lutheran
Church in 1931 made a survey in a vast suburb of

Berlin among a thousand former members who had left the Church. Not one of them recorded objections against the doctrines of the Church as a reason for cessation. The great charge was that the Church had no eye or ear for justice or for the oppressed. The Church identified only with those on the sunny side of life, who pledged their support; not high moral ideals, but self-interest dominated its attitude. The Church was on the side of the vested interest of ruling classes. Instead of rebuking or condemning their despotism and injustice, she admonished the poor and oppressed to be docile, to bear their hard burden patiently, to hope for better conditions in the hereafter, to suffer the ills of the present in order to receive the heaven of the future. Our Church in South Africa must honestly face the charges brought against her. She is too much inclined to demand support and respect of members on account of past services to the people. The city labourer wants more than this. The past leaves him cold. He wants to know what the Church does for him here and now. In former years the reverence in respect of which the Church was regarded, silenced her members even though they differed from her, but now the city dweller is much more critically inclined, and he is more candid to air his grievances. One of the most hopeful signs in our cities is that the Church is so close to the working classes. Today she is almost exclusively supported by the working classes. Today she is almost exclusively supported by the labourer, by the low paid person. These constitute her office bearers and her best members.

There are weighty reasons why the Church cannot stand aloof from the labour struggle.

● The first is because her own future is concerned with this matter. The working class will always predominantly stay in urban areas. If the Church loses her influence over them, she misses her calling; she misses her opportunity to plead their cause with the affluent and to interpret their views to others; she misses the opportunity to act as their parent and protector. If she loses their loyalty and trust, she loses exactly that class out of whom she was born, and to whom her founder belonged. If she only becomes the religious community of the higher ranks and classes, she can be assured of a peaceful yet certain death.

• The second reason is that the Church takes up a unique position in the life of the people. It is difficult to conceive of a united leadership to protect the workers. We must look for a body that is in no ways compromised to one or other viewpoint. The only one is the Church because she rises above politics. She also enjoys the trust of the people. They are already very bridle-shy of others who pose as friends but always harbour ulterior motives.

• The third reason is that it is in the interest of the spiritual case of the Church herself and that she also caters for the social economic interests of the workers who are so much exploited and extorted.

• The fourth reason is that the Christian doctrine is the best antidote to capitalism on the one hand and communism on the other. Both pay homage to a pure materialistic ideology, while Christendom proclaims the eternal truth, that man cannot live by bread alone but by God's word.

• The fifth reason is that conditions in South Africa are still redeemable. The Christian churches in Europe for many years showed no sympathy towards socialism; they preached loyalty to the king, the indispensability of class divisions, submission and patience. The socialists continuously clashed with the churches' protection of the existing established social order and with their conservatism. The result was that the Church was [preaching to] succeeding generations that were suffering the castigations of an atheistic socialism. Too late she awakened to the realization of how much right and fairness in the midst of excesses the workers had on their side, and today we find a disillusioned and penitent Church that must accept the fact that she has in a large measure lost her hold on the working classes. Our present working class in South Africa still has an inborn respect for the Church, which accounts for much in spite of attacks on religion from many sides. If a man now feels convinced in his heart that his Church is one with him in his legitimate striving for justice and protection, a new gratitude, love and loyalty towards the Church of his fathers will inspire him. The inherited respect must be supplemented and strengthened by actual experience of the Church's support and assistance, or else it may totally disappear in the second and third generation of workers. At this stage the absolute division between the new materialistic ideology and the old religion can still be avoided. The bitterness of their struggle has not yet eaten so deeply into the heart of our working classes as in other countries. The Church is still near them, among them, and co-operating with them, but what is required is the impression, the certainty among them that she is a positive support in their struggle. They have not gained this impression to the full.

Now, that is not a statement by the SACC. It is a statement made by the Dutch Reformed Church, published in a book entitled *Kerk en Stad*. It was in preparation for the Volkskongres in July 1947. It is quoted from a paper that was delivered by Dominee Dawid Botha, the Moderator of the Sendingkerk. The paper, "The Kingdom of God and the Churches in South Africa", was delivered at the National Conference of the SACC in 1980, and Dominee Botha added, in remarkable language that is bound to warm the hearts of all supporters of the liberation theologies:

In a most outstanding paper read by the Rev. C. D. Brink at the Volkskongres, the case is put even stronger. He said: "The aim of the Church is to bring about social justice. Justice must be done to the poor and oppressed, and if the present system does not serve this purpose, the public conscience must be roused to demand another. If the Church does not exert herself for justice in society, and together with the help she can offer, also be prepared to serve as champion for the cause of the poor, others will do it. The poor have their right to say: I do not ask for your charity, but I ask to be given an opportunity to live a life of human dignity."

That is a White Dutch Reformed religious leader. I do not know whether those who accuse us of being political will say that that was true of the DRC as well.

Our God does not permit us to dwell in a kind of spiritual ghetto, insulated from real life out there. Jesus used to go out and be alone with God in deep prayerful meditation, but He did not remain there. He refused to remain on the Mount of Transfiguration, but descended to the valley beneath to be involved with healing the possessed boy. He was the man for others, prodigal in the giving of Himself precisely and because He was a man of prayer, a man of God. That is our paradigm. He did not use religion as a form of escapism.

That is why He could say that we must love God and that we must love our neighbour as well, quoting from the Old Testament. These were two sides of the same coin. The one without the other was unacceptable. Love of God was authenticated and expressed in and through love of our neighbour. This is what is often referred to as the vertical dimension (relationship with God) and the horizontal dimension (relationship with our neighbour) in our Christian faith. The First Epistle of John is quite firm and unequivocal about this aspect of our Christianity: 1 John 3:15–18, 4:19–

21; and the Epistle of James 1:27; 2:14–17.

Our Lord has shocked many religious people by His parable of the Last Judgement, for here He provides a list of things the doing or the omission of which determines whether we qualify or do not qualify for Heaven, and the things He mentions could not by any stretch of the imagination be called religious in the narrow sense: feeding the hungry, clothing the naked, visiting the sick and those who are imprisoned – thoroughly mundane, secular activities – and He goes on to say that to do them to the least, the despised ones, is to do them as to Himself. Here He identifies God firmly with the downtrodden, the oppressed, the marginalized ones. And He is only being true to the nature of God as revealed in the Old Testament. The Old Testament prophets speaking on behalf of God rejected the elaborate religious ceremonies of His people. Why? Because they dealt unjustly with the poor and the powerless. Listen to some scathing words from Isaiah 1:10–17, 3–8; and from Amos 5:21–28, 7–12; 2:6–8. Elijah denounces King Ahab because his wife, Jezebel, had caused the judicial murder of a nonentity, Naboth, because the King wanted Naboth's vineyard. On behalf of God, Elijah speaks up against this tyrannical act. The prophets are deeply involved in politics because politics are the sphere where God's people demonstrate their obedience or their disobedience. The prophet Nathan rebuked King David not for a so-called religious misdemeanour but for the political act of causing the death of Bathsheba's husband.

Our religion is concerned about the here and now because that determines to a large extent the hereafter. Time in the Hebrew-Christian understanding has eternal significance, and that is why human lives and human decisions are important. All life belongs to God. The Christian faith believes that God uses ordinary material things as vehicles for God's spiritual grace and divine life, as in the sacraments.

Our religion is incarnational through and through.

William Temple, the great Archbishop of Canterbury, referring to this quality of the Christian faith said, "Christianity is the most materialistic of the great religions." We declare that we believe in the resurrection of the body and not in the immortality of the soul. The body, according to St Paul, is the temple of the Holy Spirit. Christians are not dualists who believe that matter is intrinsically evil, and therefore all God's created universe material and spiritual counts for us. The whole of life is important, political, economic and social, and none of these aspects is untouched by religion as we understand it.

It is part of God's mission and purpose for His world to bring about wholeness, justice, good health, righteousness, peace and harmony and reconciliation. These are what belong to the Kingdom of God, and we are His agents to work with Him as His partners to bring to pass all that God wants for His universe. He showed Himself as a liberator God. When He found a rabble of slaves in bondage, then because He is that kind of God, He set them free as the God of the Exodus who takes the side of the poor, the weak, the oppressed, the widow, the orphan and the alien. That is a refrain you get in the book of Deuteronomy – look after these because they represent a class in society which tends to be marginalized, to be pushed to the periphery or to the bottom of the pile, to the end of the queue. God can't help it. He always takes sides. He is not a neutral God. He takes the side of the weak and the oppressed. I am not saying so. I have shown it to be so in the Bible.

Where there is injustice, exploitation and oppression then the Bible and the God of the Bible are subversive of such a situation. Our God, unlike the pagan nature gods, is no God sanctifying the status quo. He is a God of surprises, uprooting the powerful and unjust to establish His Kingdom. We see it in the entire history of Israel.

I want to say what I have said before on another occasion: the Bible is the most revolutionary, the most radical book there is. If a book had to be banned by those who rule unjustly and as tyrants, then it ought to have been the Bible. Whites brought us the Bible and we are taking it seriously.

We are involved with God in His activity to set us all free from all that enslaves us, from all that makes us less than what He intended us to be. He sets us free to enjoy the glorious liberty of the children of God. And all our work is consistent with the Gospel of Jesus, the Gospel of God's love and God's compassion and God's reconciling and forgiving grace.

Our Home and Family Life Division is concerned about the sanctity of marriage and family life. Is that not something pleasing to God in a country that has Family Day as one of its national holidays and then one of the highest divorce rates in the world? We are involved, in this Division, with the causes and the remedies for juvenile delinquency and illegitimacy. The Division is concerned about the status of women and their role in society. Our health educator is seeking to help mothers and others in depressed communities with proper feeding and health care. It all has to do with the wholeness of the Kingdom of God.

The pastoral work of the SACC
Our Division of Inter-Church Aid is deeply involved with community development schemes, helping people to feed themselves and to become more self-reliant. We provide relief in drought-stricken areas and other areas of natural and human disaster. We found money from the worldwide Church, through the World Council of Churches, to contribute R10,000 to the Laingsberg Flood Disaster fund. We help to provide boreholes in arid areas and encourage garden projects. We supply blankets to the needy, the infirm and the aged, especially through funds we get during the

August Month of Compassion sponsored by the Division. We put into action our words about love for our neighbour. Can anybody rightly describe any of the work I have so far described as anything but truly Christlike and obeying His command to love our neighbour as ourselves? Could anyone in his right mind want to criticize this or any of our other work as destabilizing? Are we not helping to establish a healthy community in a more just society, that is truly democratic and non-racial?

We in the SACC do many things that in more normal countries would be the responsibility of the State. For instance, each year we help to educate a thousand pupils at high school in rural areas, and we give a hundred new bursaries annually for university and technical education. In other societies we would be lauded for this outstanding work. In our beloved country we are vilified, harassed and abused. Mercifully we do none of all this work to be praised by men. We do it because we are under divine constraint – as St Paul exclaimed of himself, "Woe is me if I preach not the Gospel." Woe are we if we do not obey that Gospel, to serve God and Christ by serving Him in the least of His brethren. We help to defuse an explosive and volatile situation through our Unemployment Project. In a time of high unemployment the SACC is engaged nationwide in encouraging the unemployed to be involved in self-employment and self-help projects, and yet we are accused of undermining the stability of society. On the other side we have often been attacked for delaying the bloody revolution through these self-help projects. Again we play to no gallery, we do what we believe is right and in accord with the Gospel of Jesus Christ.

In obedience to Christ's command, we care for political prisoners, detainees and banned persons as well as for their families and dependants, especially through our Dependants' Conference. We help to arrange for family visits to political prisoners. What is so sinister about that?

Why are our Dependants' Conference fieldworkers so often detained by the police? We are determined to continue with this and similar work, for we had much rather obey God than man. Why are we in the SACC treated as if this country was somewhere behind the Iron Curtain and Christians must behave as if they were conspirators, when what we are doing is in fact above board and out in the open for everyone to see?

I operate a fund, the Asingeni Fund, at my total discretion, from which I pay the legal costs of people charged with political offences. I should in a normal country be praised for helping with the administration of proper justice, since we claim that it is the right of each person to have the best possible defence. If it is a crime to do all these things I am more than happy, indeed proud to plead guilty to the crime. But I want to declare here, as forthrightly as I can, that we will continue to do this work come hell or high water.

Let me refer again to our Division of Justice and Reconciliation. It tries to keep the public and the churches informed on sensitive and critical issues such as nationalism, foreign investment, uprooting and dumping in forced population removals, the Mixed Marriages and Immorality Acts, Bantustan policy, political ideologies, e.g. Marxism, communism, etc. And we are heavily involved in matters of justice (a biblical concern as we showed) because we believe that real reconciliation can never happen before justice is established. We showed that the Bible and the God of the Bible were destabilizers where injustice, oppression, alienation held sway. The SACC is basically law-abiding and concerned for justice and peace, for reconciliation and unity. But in a real sense because we are opposed to injustice and oppression, we cannot support a system where these are found, and to seek to change such a system even by reasonably peaceful means is to be a destabilizing factor in such a society. We want to dismantle apartheid, and the perpetrators of apartheid don't like that at all. They could hardly regard us as blue-eyed boys because the privilege they enjoy as a result of apartheid is threatened. And so we have the total onslaught of the apartheid machinery turned against us.

Our commitment to dialogue

We are concerned to work for a new kind of South Africa, a non-racial, truly democratic and more just society, by reasonably peaceful means. We as a Council deplore all forms of violence, and have said so times without number. We deplore structural and legalized violence that maintains an unjust socio-political dispensation, and the violence of those who would overthrow the State. But we have consistently warned too that oppressed people will become desperate, and desperate people will use desperate methods.

We have a Commission on Violence and Non-Violence, and are concerned about the increasing militarization of our land, and believe that conscientious objectors should be given alternative forms of national service as in most normal societies. We believe in negotiation, discussion and dialogue. That is why in 1980 we had discussions with the Government to try to arrange for the Government to meet with the authentic leaders of all sections of South African society (for Blacks it would include political prisoners and those in exile), and that is why we call still for a national convention.

I myself believe in dialogue and meeting. I have spoken at all the Afrikaans university campuses, including that of the Orange Free State. In fact the only White university campus at which I have not spoken is the University of Port Elizabeth. I have spoken to some mainly Afrikaans organizations and groups such as *Peil 2000* and *POLSTU*. That could not be the attitude of someone out for confrontation, could it? Many in the Black community ask why I still waste my time talking to Whites, and I tell them that our mandate is biblical. Moses went to Pharaoh several times even when he knew that it was futile. The prophets addressed the kings of Israel time and time again because they were to deliver the message faithfully even if they were being rejected.

The National Conference of the SACC in June 1982 declared apartheid a heresy and said we should have no further dialogue with the DRC until it denounces apartheid as evil. But I want to tell you that we reached this point only after several efforts at holding out a hand of fellowship to the NGK. In 1978 I reminded Dr Geldenhuys, then its ecumenical officer and later its Chief Executive Officer, that my predecessor had written on behalf of our Executive Committee to invite the NGK to send an observer to its meeting and not on a reciprocal basis. He replied to say that his Synod had turned down our invitation. Then we said: Do not let it be an official observer; let it be an unofficial observer; it need not be a mutual arrangement. We do not ask to appoint or allow someone from the SACC to sit on your meetings. He wrote back to say that even this invitation had been rejected.

But nothing daunted, we went on; we invited them to participate in a consultation on racism in 1980, at Hammanskraal. They did not even reply to my letter, except by statements in the press. The consultation at Hammanskraal was quite angry at this action of the Dutch Reformed Churches. But I asked the permission of the consultation; I said I felt that I was under divine constraint to write to the NGK saying that they should please forgive us of the SACC and its member churches for anything we had done to hurt them in the past, but that we believe that nothing substantial would happen in this country to change its unjust structures, unless that powerful and mighty church were to be involved. A small delegation from the Dutch Reformed Church came to see me in what they said must be a totally confidential meeting.

So we have tried to engage them in dialogue, and we have

been rebuffed. What more could we do? We are sad at what has happened to them in Ottawa. We do not gloat, and we continue to pray for their conversion, because, and this is my pet theory, once an Afrikaner sees the light of Jesus Christ as other people see it, there is no stopping him, for there are no half-measures with him. When an Afrikaner is committed, and committed to the Gospel of Jesus Christ, then he is committed to the hilt.

We of the South African Council of Churches belong to the Church of God, the one holy, Catholic, Apostolic church. What it means is that we belong to something quite tremendous. Those who are for us are many times more than those against us. We belong to this remarkable fellowship, so that we can receive a letter, as we have done, from a Lutheran pastor in Alaska assuring us that he and his congregation are praying for us. When I lost my passport for the first time, I was overwhelmed by messages of sympathy and support from all over the world, but nothing touched me more than to get from the Sunday School children at St James, Madison Avenue in New York, what the children called passports of love, which I pasted up on the walls of my office. How can anyone range himself against this international, this global fellowship?

I want to stress what I said in the preamble: the Church is made up of frail, fallible human beings, and that is true also for the SACC. In the New Testament we hear Our Lord's parable of the Kingdom concerning the wheat and tares. That is a picture, too, of the Church, which is an agent for the Kingdom. The Church is the home of sinners and the school for saints. We always marvel that God can want to use such unworthy creatures as we know ourselves to be. His treasure, St Paul tells us, is held in us, who are but earthenware vessels, so that the abounding glory should belong rightly where it belongs; not to us, but to God.

I have shown that the teaching which we proclaim, which is under scrutiny by this Commission, is based squarely and truly on the Bible. But it is also in line with the teaching of the Church of God throughout the world. It is a fact of life, that can be noted by anyone who has eyes to see and does want to see, who is not biased, that the South African Council of Churches enjoys the support of the overwhelming segment of the Christian community in the world. I am not aware that, for instance, the Dutch Reformed Church, which supports apartheid, enjoys even a fraction of the support we enjoy. I am not boasting; I am just stating a fact. In fact some people criticize us because we have this support, expressed in money gifts to us.

Why do we enjoy such worldwide support? It is possible to deceive some people all the time, but surely we could not be endowed with the ability to deceive such a large body of responsible and mature Christians for so long. We have operated and we continue to operate openly. We report regularly to our member churches, through our National Conference and at every quarterly meeting of our Executive Committee, on which the churches are represented, and they have on the whole been satisfied so far. We do not operate secretly, and yet there are private, secret societies in this land which are alleged – I do not know whether this is true – which are alleged to exercise an enormous influence on some churches and on political leaders, and yet such secret societies are not, to my knowledge, investigated. We do not receive funds clandestinely. They are recorded openly, and yet there are organizations, even religious organizations, some of which were involved in the Information Scandal, which have received clandestine funding, and were set up precisely to undermine a legitimate body such as the SACC, and those sinister organizations are not investigated but continue with impunity to spew forth their poisonous filth. A bank recently lost over a million rand through the malfeasance of one of its employees. The court found that she had in fact been assisted by other bank officials, and yet I have not heard that that bank, which deals with far more of the public's funds than the SACC could ever hope to do, I have not heard that that bank is being investigated by any commission. Why not, if we are?

We are told that we do not enjoy the support of the churches in South Africa. That statement may be true, to some extent, if we mean by South African churches the White part of the Church. In our membership by and large, White Christians form only 20 per cent of our constituency. The Black membership, forming nearly 80 per cent of our constituency, can be said without fear of contradiction to represent that part of the Church that supports the SACC to a very considerable extent. But even if this were not the case, Our Lord has warned us that we must beware when all men speak well of us.

The SACC has acted as mediators in labour disputes, and did so successfully in the Fattis and Monis strike. The SACC, dreaming about what this country has it in her to become, sponsored what was called a "Pilgrimage of Hope", consisting of young people and not quite so young people, 144 of them, who went on a pilgrimage of hope. They were children of all races, and went to the Holy Land, to Switzerland, and then to Taizé, whose massive church is called the Church of Reconciliation. We hoped, we said, that by this we are demonstrating to South Africa our hope that these young people, roughing, loving, playing, praying together, will come back and be able to demonstrate that the Church of God is a foreshadowing, a first-fruits of what South Africa will become.

I think it is important to state that we in the SACC believe absolutely in the centrality of the spiritual; that we are not just a bunch of activist do-gooders engaged in the social gospel. We have as our example and paradigm the Son of God

Himself, who spent whole nights in prayer, had retreats, and then concerned Himself to meet human need. What we do and say stems from our encounter with God and Our Lord Jesus Christ, at worship, in Bible study, in meditation, and in the Eucharist.

M'Lord, you will not find any SACC staff members in their offices if you come to Khotso House at half past eight every morning, because we are in chapel, every day. Every Wednesday at lunch time we have prayers for justice and reconciliation in our land, and some of us have a fast on Thursdays for the same purpose. Once a month we celebrate the Eucharist according to the rite of one or other of our member churches. We start our two-day quarterly Executive Committee meetings with a substantial Bible study, and have a Eucharist with a homily on the second day. Both the executive and non-executive staff have an annual week-long retreat. We have a daily Eucharist, substantial daily Bible studies as features of every National Conference. Before each National Conference I write to religious communities in this country and abroad, asking for their prayers for the conference, which is thus surrounded by a considerable volume of prayer.

As a Bishop of the Church, I am under obligation to pray the Office of the Church twice a day. I want to say that for me the most important – the most cardinal – fact about our life is the spiritual: that encounter with God in prayer, in worship, in meditation.

I am sorry to reveal this secret part of our lives, which Scripture exhorts must not be paraded before men. I have been compelled to talk about it, to show that we try to be persons of prayer, people who try to wait on Our Lord. We may not always hear Him aright, and often perhaps when we hear what He says, we do not like what He is asking us to do, but I want to assure you that we are not politicians. We are attempting to be devout Christians. Speaking for

186

myself, I want to say that there is nothing the Government can do to me that will stop me from being involved in what I believe is what God wants me to do. I do not do it because I like doing it. I do it because I am under what I believe to be the influence of God's hand. I cannot help it: when I see injustice I cannot keep quiet. I will not keep quiet, for, as Jeremiah says, when I try to keep quiet, God's word burns like a fire in my breast. But what is it that they can ultimately do? The most awful thing that they can do is to kill me, and death is not the worst thing that could happen to a Christian.

Our Lord has tried to weld us into a family: people of different races, who demonstrate, however feebly and fitfully, what this beautiful land can be. If only we could begin to treat people as persons created by God in His image, redeemed by Jesus Christ and sanctified by the Holy Spirit. What a wonderful land it would be; and we believe that it will happen, in fulfilment of that magnificent vision in the Revelation of St John the Divine, chapter 7, verse 9.

Of course, it cannot happen without suffering and anguish. Jesus did not promise His followers a bed of roses. On the contrary, and central to it all, was the inevitability and unavoidable nature of suffering. It could be said from this that a Church that does not suffer, cannot be the Church of Jesus Christ. I do not mean we should be masochists. Suffering will seek us out. It is part of the divine economy of salvation.

Interestingly enough, M'Lord, in the Anglican calendar this week we are bidden to think of the Church as the suffering community, and this is the special prayer for this week:

God Our Loving Father, You gave Your only Son to suffer and to die for me. Grant that when we are found worthy to endure suffering for Christ's name, we may rejoice in our calling and be enabled to bear our part in completing His sufferings for the sake of Your Church.

We are not to be surprised at suffering that comes to us because of witnessing for the Kingdom of God and for the Gospel of Jesus Christ. Listen to these words of Our Lord:

If the world hates you, it hated Me first, as you know well. If you belong to the world, the world would love its own, but because you do not belong to the world, because I have chosen you out of the world, for that reason the world hates you. Remember what I said: a servant is not greater than his master. As they persecuted Me, they will persecute you. They will follow your teachings as little as they have followed Mine. It is on My account that they will treat you thus, because they do not know the one who sent Me.

And in Matthew chapter 10:17–22:

Be on your guard, for men will hand you over to their courts; they will flog you in their synagogues and you will be brought before governors and kings for My sake, to testify before them and the heathen, but when you are arrested, do not worry about what you are to say. When the time comes, the words you need will be given you, for it is not you who will be speaking. It will be the Spirit of your Father speaking in you. Brother will betray brother to death and the father his child; children will turn against their parents and send them to their death. All will hate you for your allegiance to Me, but the man who holds out to the end, will be saved.

God's purposes are certain. They may remove a Tutu; they may remove the South African Council of Churches, but

God's intention to establish His Kingdom of justice, of love, of compassion, will not be thwarted. We are not scared, certainly not of the Government, or any other perpetrators of injustice and oppression, for victory is ours through Him who loved us.

I end, M'Lord and members of the Commission. "With all this in mind, what are we to say? If God is on our side, who is against us? . . . What can separate us from the love of Christ? Can affliction or hardship? Can persecution, hunger, nakedness, peril or the sword? 'We are being done to death for Thy sake all day long' as Scripture says: 'we have been treated like sheep for slaughter' – and yet, in spite of all, overwhelming victory is ours through Him who loved us. For I am convinced that there is nothing in death or life, in the realm of spirits or superhuman powers, in the world as it is or the world as it shall be, in the forces of the universe, in heights or depths – nothing in all creation that can separate us from the love of God in Christ Jesus Our Lord." Thank you.

Presentation to the Eloff Commission of Inquiry
1 September 1982